GEORGE W. WARE

GERMAN AND AUSTRIAN PORCELAIN

GEORGE W. WARE

German and Austrian

Porcelain

CROWN PUBLISHERS, INC., NEW YORK

Cover and Title by Hermann Zapf

Unabridged German Version by Mrs. Wilhelmine Woeller-Paquet

Published by the Lothar Woeller Press
Kriftel (Taunus) near Frankfurt-Main, Western Germany
Under the Title of
Deutsches und Oesterreichisches Porzellan

This edition published by Crown Publishers, Inc.,
by arrangement with the original publisher.

Inquiries should be addressed to Crown Publishers, Inc.,
One Park Avenue, New York, N.Y. 10016
Library of Congress Catalog Card Number: 77-79320
ISBN: 0-517-52323X
Printed in the United States of America
Published simultaneously in Canada by
General Publishing Company Limited
Third Printing, June, 1977

INTRODUCTION

Although George McClellan's vivid guide to his collection of German and Austrian porcelain in 1946, and Louise Avery's fine catalogue of the European porcelain exhibition in New York in 1949 are landmarks signifying the growing interest for German porcelain in this part of the world, this book on the subject by an American newcomer is really the first one of greater importance in the United States. Compared with the two standard works in the English language by Hannover and Honey, London, 1925 and 1947 respectively, it has a refreshing approach and involves a systematic and unique handling of the material.

The author of this book, George W. Ware, was for seventeen years in charge of the University of Arkansas Horticultural Experiment Station. His interest as an amateur ceramics collector was greatly increased when he became more acquainted with German porcelain and enthusiastic about its beauty and individuality during his six years' residence as an agricultural and educational adviser in the American Zone of Germany, following World War II. As a hobby during his spare time, he studied and collected the little delicate objects d'art of 18th century spirit, read many books on the subject, consulted experts, visited museums and art galleries, private collections and porcelain factories. He gathered with a keen sense and tasteful understanding a rare knowledge that enabled him to write this very useful and inspiring book which has also been published in the German language.

Although the author states that his book is written mainly for people who are starting to collect this kind of porcelain or who want a quick unsophisticated survey on the subject, he can pride himself that his publication is helpful in every respect and informative even to the connoisseur and so-called expert. Not only are historical parts well outlined and abounding with necessary information, but the practical chapters are also useful for everyone. Most helpful is the section on the 19th and 20th century productions and the collection of newly drawn marks which brings our knowledge up-to-date. The charming reproductions, carefully selected and well-balanced, enhance and enliven the text. The number and variety of objects brought to public light by the author's zeal and understanding will not only stimulate amateur collectors but connoisseurs as well.

In introducing this subject, we may ask why the interest and delight in German 18th century porcelain has increased so greatly in this country within recent years. The spirit of the Rococo is remote from our concept of life, and the aristocratic background before which these gay and frivolous fragilities moved appears to our realistic, mechanically minded age to be from another world. However, the porcelain figurines and groups and the delicately-painted tablewares of that period reveal definite qualities which strongly appeal to the modern spirit. The clarity and precision of form, the translucence of the nearly weightless material, and the liveliness of the glazed surface reflect the mind and taste of the 18th century which we are just rediscovering in relation to our own. It is possible to associate our recognition of these qualities with the revived enthusiasm for the music of Haydn and Mozart which is at present sweeping the country.

The author is to be congratulated on this outstanding international art book which will certainly help to arouse and increase interest in a field that, in spite of some earlier attempts, has been so overlooked and neglected in the United States until recently.

Dr. Oswald Goetz
The Art Institute of Chicago

FOREWORD

This book was written by an amateur porcelain collector to help other collectors in their search for artistic porcelain. It was prepared primarily for the information and guidance of those with limited experience rather than for the expert. Advanced collectors or museum ceramics curators, however, should find it a convenient, authentic, and up-to-date reference book and general guide.

Porcelain is only one segment of the whole field of ceramics. In addition, when the geographical limitations of German and Austrian porcelain are recognized, there results what may appear to be a limited subject upon which to write. One must also realize that the period of artistic excellence of German and Austrian porcelain, like that of other European countries, is confined to a brief period, only about sixty years during the middle part of the 18th century. The importance of this subject, however, rests in the fact that the first true porcelain of Europe was made in Germany, and that the early German and Austrian factories set the pattern for hard-paste porcelain production throughout the Western World. Consequently, early German porcelain has considerable artistic and historical importance and material value. The first Far Eastern creations were soon replaced by prevailing fashions of the West, and the history and development of German and Austrian porcelain are closely associated with the tastes and whims of its royal patrons.

The author of this book took advantage of several years' residence in Germany to develop as a spare-time hobby his long-standing interest in porcelain. For him, his wife, Dorothy, and his son, George, this study involves more than a book. It is also an account of fascinating visits to museums, interesting conversations with experts of porcelain factories, and exciting discoveries in many out-of-the-way antique shops. Subsequently visits to museums and with collectors and dealers in Latin American and other capitals reveal universal appreciation of this subject. The willingness and patience of curators, manufacturers, collectors and dealers to share their knowledge have made this publication possible.

The writer was particularly fortunate in enjoying a long and close acquaintance with Professor Martin Klar, Director of the Schlossmuseum, Berlin, one of the few great surviving porcelain authorities in Germany. He was a real inspiration and, as a severe critic, he revealed the fundamentals of artistic porcelain as only a master could do. Also to Dr. E. W. Braun, a distinguished author and art expert of the Germanisches National-Museum, Nürnberg, the writer is indebted for valuable assistance in preparing the porcelain marks and in supplying historical information. Mrs. Wilhelmine Woeller-Paquet deserves particular credit for her preparation of a separately-published unabridged German version of this book, and for her general composition and editorial contributions.

The author wishes to especially acknowledge the valuable assistance provided by such authoritative works on the subject as "German Porcelain" by Mr. H. B. Honey, published by Faber and Faber Limited of London. Mr. Honey's book on the identical subject was an inspiration and valuable source of information and reference.

Appreciation is also extended to Dr. Oswald Goetz of the Art Institute of Chicago, a leading American expert on porcelain, who checked the manuscript and prepared the Introduction; and to Miss C. Louise Avery, Associate Curator of The Metropolitan Museum of Art, New York; Mr. Louis C. Madeira, Assistant Curator of The Philadelphia Museum of Art; Mr. G. Ryland Scott, an outstanding collector and lecturer; and to Drs. William L. Wrinkle and Edgar Breitenbach for their literary and technical suggestions.

Acknowledgement is made of the valuable assistance received from Director Rudolf Lunghard of the Porcelain Technical Institute at Selb; and the kindness of Dr. Arno Schönberger, ceramics curator of the Bayerisches Nationalmuseum, Munich; Count Solms-Laubach, Director of the Museum für Kunsthandwerk, Frankfurt; and Drs. Kurt Dingelstedt and Martin Feddersen, ceramics curators of the Museum für Kunst und Gewerbe, Hamburg, all of whom read the manuscript, offered valuable suggestions and supplied pictures of outstanding porcelain. Also appreciation is extended to Dr. Eugen Eberhardt for his research and technical translations, and to Mrs. Hildegard Pankratz for copying the manuscripts.

This statement would be incomplete if attention was not called to the valuable aid which museums, manufacturers and collectors rendered in supplying photographs, historical information and technical data which added materially to the contents and authenticity of the book.

George W. Ware

CONTENTS

CHAPTER IV

OTHER PORCELAIN FACTORIES

CHAPTER V

SUGGESTIONS FOR THE AMATEUR

APPENDIX

ILLUSTRATIONS

COLORED PLATES

MISCELLANEOUS PICTURES

CHARTS AND MAPS

PORCELAIN MARKS

BLACK AND WHITE REPRODUCTIONS

GEORGE W. WARE

GERMAN AND AUSTRIAN PORCELAIN

CHAPTER I

General History of Porcelain

The word "porcelain" is derived from "*porcella*" because of its similarity to the smooth white cowry sea shells which are called *porcella* in several languages. Porcelain, commonly referred to as "china" by most English-speaking peoples, is universally admired and collected by many persons of all races and circumstances. Although technically the manufacture of porcelain is classified as an applied art, its finest specimens rank with classical paintings and sculpture as a collector's joy. Because of its many sources, ages, forms and qualities, porcelain is acquired for artistic or practical purposes in greater abundance perhaps than any other item for the home. It appears in countless forms — from great chandeliers to miniature buttons, from magnificent table services to humble ash trays, from life-size monuments to small artistic figures. A great variety of items, almost anything that one desires, has been or can be made in porcelain. Indeed, it is a subject of unusual interest. History, economics, politics, science, geography, superstition and intrigue are all interwoven with the discovery and development of porcelain which has captured the fancy of noblemen and common people throughout the world.

Man has known the art of molding things out of clay and hardening them in the fire since prehistoric times; however, it was a long time before porcelain, "china," was first made by the Chinese. Some authorities believe that it was produced as early as the Sui Dynasty (581-617 AD), while others claim that Chinese porcelain was first perfected during the T'ang period (618-906). The excavations of Samarra prove conclusively that porcelain was made before 800 AD, but the exact date of its discovery remains a matter of conjecture. It is known, however, that it was not suddenly invented but was developed and refined over a long period of time. The secret of making "china" or porcelain was learned subsequently by the Japanese and Koreans, but it remained a mystery to the rest of the world for several centuries.

Marco Polo, the Venetian traveler who visited the Court of China between 1271 and 1295, was one of the first Europeans to describe Chinese porcelain. Limited quantities were brought overland for the noble and rich of Europe, but it was not until after the discovery of the sea route around the Cape of Good Hope in 1497 that Far Eastern porcelain became an article of foreign commerce.

There had been a long search throughout the Western world for food and liquid containers which were low-heat conductors, easy to clean, non-porous and free from the flavor taint which is imparted by earthenware and metal vessels. Since porcelain satisfied all of the desired requirements, its popularity became widespread.

According to F. H. Hofmann, coffee houses, which were often referred to as "Houses of Wisdom," were introduced in Turkey and Egypt in the 16th century and spread successively to Italy, England, France and Germany in the last half of the 17th century. Chocolate houses also flourished, and there was a large demand for porcelain cups, saucers and accessories as stoneware did not meet the requirements for these beverages. As general economic conditions improved following the Thirty Years War (1618-1648), personal taste demanded general improvement and refinement in ornamental and useful wares. Consequently, an extreme desire for porcelain developed in German-speaking provinces and other European countries. To meet this growing demand, the various East India Companies, encouraged by the Manchu Emperor K'ang Hsi (1662-1722),* shipped large quantities of Chinese porcelain that had been made and specially decorated according to Western European taste to Germany, Holland and other countries. Despite large Eastern importations and the production in Europe of considerable quantities in the 18th century and later, porcelain became generally available to peoples of ordinary circumstances only during the last hundred and fifty years or so.

Since porcelain proved to be an ideal medium for tablewares and decorative items, its popularity became so widespread that potters throughout Europe raced to solve the mystery of its composition in order to capture the market. Porcelain was widely imitated in various forms of glazed porous wares in Frankfurt, Hanau,

*Dates in parentheses refer to the life span of the individual unless otherwise indicated.

14

Nürnberg and several other cities in Germany as well as in Holland, Italy and France. Several legendary successes were reported in Italy, and a very limited quantity of pseudo-porcelain was made at Florence under the Medici in the years 1575 to 1620. Although some soft-paste porcelain was produced in France at ROUEN* from 1673 to 1696, the first successful soft-paste porcelain factory opened at SAINT CLOUD around 1696 and operated until about 1773. Other French soft-paste porcelain factories sprang up in rapid succession at LILLE in 1711, CHANTILLY in 1725, and MENNECY VILLEROY in 1735. Then came the most successful of all, VINCENNES, 1738, and its successor, SEVRES, in 1756. It was not until later in the second half of the 18th century that French factories learned to make a satisfactory hard-paste porcelain.

Although soft-paste porcelain is beautiful and preferred by many, it does not have the strength and endurance of true or hard-paste porcelain which dominated many markets soon after its discovery. The various types of porcelain and other ceramics are described on pages 30, 35, 37 and 38 and in the Glossary.

THE GREAT DISCOVERY AT MEISSEN

The European nobility, the greatest Western patrons of Chinese porcelain, did much to stimulate the discovery and development of a similar product in Europe. The interest of royalty in porcelain and other exotic ornamentals was a natural development in this period of history, when the grandeur of royal pomp was in its ascendancy and each of the courts was trying to excel the others.

The energetic art-loving monarch, August the Strong (1670-1733), Elector of Saxony and King of Poland, deserves indirect credit for the discovery of true porcelain on the European continent. An ardent admirer and collector of Chinese and Japanese porcelain, it is reported that he spent so much of his wealth collecting ornamental porcelain and beautifying his palaces that he became desperate and sought some method to replenish his treasury and satisfy his craze for porcelain. The King reasoned that a porcelain factory of his own would do both, so in 1706

*The names of porcelain factories appear in BOLD-FACE TYPE throughout the book in order to distinguish them from cities and other similar proper names.

he secured the assistance of E. W. von Tschirnhaus,* an eminent mathematician and scientist, provided him with research personnel and equipment, and encouraged him in various ways to do everything possible to discover a method of producing porcelain—the material of his love and ambition.

In the meantime, August the Strong heard of an astonishing young alchemist, Johann Friedrich Böttger (1682-1719), who was reputed to be making gold from base metals. When Böttger fled from Berlin to avoid the Prussian King who desired his exclusive services, he was seized by agents of August the Strong and brought to Dresden as a prisoner and was confined in the near-by Albrechtsburg castle at Meissen. In desperation, August "ordered" Böttger to produce gold which was urgently needed to meet the mounting debts and expenses of State. Böttger naturally failed in his efforts to make gold but he convinced the King that with patience and good luck he might be able to produce porcelain. With the equipment and able assistance of Tschirnhaus, and after repeated experiments, Böttger finally produced, in 1708, the year Tschirnhaus died, the hardest stoneware ever made, *Böttger Steinzeug* (Figs. 1 and 2).** The next year true porcelain with a glaze was made, and by 1710 white porcelain, *Böttger Porzellan* (Figs. 3 and 4), was available for the King's inspection. August the Strong forthwith decreed the establishment of a royal porcelain factory at Dresden on January 23, 1710, under the direction of Böttger (Page 42). For security reasons the factory was moved to the Albrechtsburg castle at Meissen on June 6 of the same year. By 1713 pieces from the MEISSEN factory were offered for sale at the Leipzig Fair. Thus to Böttger goes the direct credit and glory of discovering true porcelain in Europe, although some authorities are inclined to believe that Tschirnhaus is more responsible for its invention. At any rate, by methodically fusing all kinds of clay, they produced a material which proved to be a source of gold for the king's depleted coffers and at the same time afforded him the great pleasure and prestige of owning the first hard-paste porcelain factory in Europe. Böttger was so pleased with the discovery that he appropriately inscribed over the door of his laboratory: *"It Pleased the Lord to Change a Gold-maker into a Potter."*

*The names and initials of persons which vary greatly in the several books are spelled herein according to F. H. Hofmann's "Das Porzellan," 1932, which is conceded to be one of the most authentic guides.

**Figure numbers which appear in parentheses throughout the text refer to the illustrations which appear numerically in the last section of the book. Foreign terms are italicized and many are found in the Glossary.

The discovery of porcelain opened up a new, exciting and competitive field. Every precaution was taken to prevent the *arcanum* (the Latin word for secret) from falling into the hands of spies and unscrupulous persons who were interested in opening competitive factories. The employees were sworn to "secrecy to death," and deaf and dumb workers are reputed to have been employed and held as virtual prisoners in order to prevent the secret formula from escaping the walls of the factory. Suspicion, jealousy, distrust and hate prevailed. Threats, bribery, alcohol, seduction and other devices of deceit and violence were employed to obtain the secret or *arcanum*. Although constant vigilance and precaution were maintained, Samuel Stöltzel, who had left MEISSEN "without leave," assisted in starting production in the Du Paquier VIENNA factory in 1718. Konrad Christoph Hunger, also a deserter from MEISSEN, carried the secret to the VENICE enterprise in 1720. These factories did not offer serious competition to MEISSEN which was well established and continued to dominate the porcelain industry until about 1756.

The "spreading of the secret" had only begun. Hunger became a roving *arcanist* upon leaving VENICE. His secret formuae were often copied by his drinking companions. He offered his services to potters in Germany, Austria and Sweden and worked as a private decorator of porcelain when out of a factory job. He was last heard of in 1748 when he was expelled from Russia after he had given the ST. PETERSBURG factory advantage of his knowledge.

Strange as it may seem, no outstanding hard-paste porcelain factories developed for almost 30 years following the establishment of the VIENNA factory in 1718. However, in 1749, Joseph Jakob Ringler who had gained the *arcanum* through the friendship of the daughter of Du Paquier, first proprietor of the VIENNA factory, deserted from that establishment and aided in developing or improving the methods of such important factories as HÖCHST, about 1750; STRASBOURG, 1751, whose manager Paul Anton Hannong founded the FRANKENTHAL factory in 1755; NYMPHENBURG in 1753-1757; and a number of minor factories in the meantime. H. B. Honey* states, "Ringler then went on to help in the establishment of the

---

*When authors are quoted, their statements appear in "quotation Marks," and their names and publications are listed in the Bibliography on pages 227 and 228.

LUDWIGSBURG factory, also in Württemberg, where he also settled down, remaining manager from 1759 until 1802, two years before his death.

Ringler's associate at Künersberg and Höchst, Johann Benckgraff, sold the 'arcanum' or secret of porcelain, first in 1752 to a manufacture proposed at BERLIN by a wool-merchant named Wegely, and in 1753 to that at FÜRSTENBERG in Brunswick where he died the same year.

Last among the wandering arcanists should be mentioned Nikolaus Paul, who received the secret from Reichard at Berlin in 1755, and was also from 1757 to 1760 at Fürstenberg (whence be offered his services to GOTHA and HÖXTER), before starting factories in turn at WEESP in Holland (1764), FULDA (1764-65), CASSEL (1767) and abortively at PASSAU (1776). He was later at KLOSTER VEILSDORF in Thuringia (1766-68)."

MEISSEN workers betrayed the secret so often that it became almost common knowledge. However, if it were not for the restless, wandering so-called deserters such as Stöltzel, Hunger, Ringler, Benckgraff and Paul, the MEISSEN establishment might have monopolized the porcelain industry for a much longer period of time, thereby depriving the masses of possessing porcelain and requiring them to continue using simpler forms of pottery, wood and metal for household and utility and decorative purposes.

DEVELOPMENT OF AN INTERNATIONAL INDUSTRY

MEISSEN developed into a highly successful enterprise for August the Strong, and stimulated widespread interest in porcelain. The VIENNA factory, which was established in 1718, came under the management of the Austrian State, in 1744, and received the enthusiastic sponsorship of Empress Maria Theresa. The production of porcelain became such a vogue among the royalty that each family prince aspired to establish his own factory for prestige and potential revenue. European rulers vied ardently with each other for position and leadership in the competition of "white gold." They offered their royal patronage not only in the establishment but also in the operation of the several manufactories. Of the eight major establishments, six were organized with the assistance of Electors, the ruling princes and prince-bishops of the German provinces who selected the Emperor. The Province Electors of Mainz, Bavaria, and the Palatinate, and the King of Prussia respectively established the major factories of HÖCHST, 1746; NYMPHENBURG, 1753, FRANKENTHAL, 1755; and BERLIN in 1763, all of which began to challenge the supremacy which MEISSEN had held. Several other factories were started by princes not bearing the title of Elector. For example, Duke Karl I of Brunswick founded the FÜRSTENBERG factory which started producing in 1753; and the Duke of Württemberg, Karl Eugen, started the LUDWIGSBURG factory in 1758. Between 1758 and 1775, princes and prince-bishops also started or patronized the small but important factories of ANSBACH, KELSTERBACH, OTTWEILER, FULDA, KASSEL, GUTENBRUNN, and WÜRZBURG (Pages 78 to 82).

Under the initial encouragement and assistance of royal patronage, porcelain production had grown into a great international industry. By the end of the 18th century Germany and Austria had eight major factories, and more than twenty smaller ones which had developed primarily in Thuringia, Saxony, and other parts of Germany where there was an abundance of raw materials. Similarly, a number of state or private porcelain factories had been established in France, England, Italy, Russia, and several other European countries as shown on the map, page 41.

Since European hard-paste porcelain was first manufactured at MEISSEN, the German style and method of production dominated or influenced a number of porcelain factories in other European countries. For example, the Alsatian factories STRASBOURG, 1745; and NIEDERWEILER, 1768, were completely under German influence. Italy's VENICE, 1720; Russia's ST. PETERSBURG, 1744; ZÜRICH of Switzerland, 1763; and WEESP and THE HAGUE of Holland, 1764 and 1775, respectively; COPENHAGEN, Denmark, 1772; and MARIEBERG, Sweden, 1780, were either managed by German directors for varying periods of time or were under German influence. In turn, German establishments had been originally influenced by the Chinese and Japanese and later by the fashions and techniques of such factories as SEVRES and COPENHAGEN.

It is interesting to note that in practically all instances the old factories in Germany and elsewhere bear the names of the cities in which they were situated. MEISSEN, VIENNA, HÖCHST, FÜRSTENBERG, BERLIN, FRANKENTHAL, LUDWIGSBURG, ANSBACH; and SEVRES, STRASBOURG, BRISTOL, NAPLES,

VENICE, COPENHAGEN, WEESP, BRUSSELS, PRAGUE, LISBON, MADRID and
ST. PETERSBURG are typical examples.

THE ART AND STYLES OF PORCELAIN

Honey reports that: "The art of porcelain, in Germany as well as the rest of
eighteenth-century Europe, was essentially a luxury art, depending on the patronage of the wealthy class, remote from all concern with the harsher realities
of existence ... Porcelain was then felt to be an exciting and almost precious
substance. To make it and fashion it into amusing and delightful shapes and to
employ upon it every available resource of the color-chemist and painter was the
ambition of every potter." Consequently, outstanding modelers and painters were
pressed into service to satisfy the whims of their noble and rich clientele. The
making of porcelain was considered a plastic art calling upon the creative gift and
aesthetic sense of the modelers and guilders. The artists produced many beautiful
and highly decorative pieces which have never been excelled. They used every
form and color combination which would enhance artistic value.

The first European hard-paste porcelain which was produced at MEISSEN had
no characteristic style of its own. The brown and white pieces made by Böttger
between 1710 and 1719 were fashioned after silver, metal and stone models.
Johann J. Irminger, the first porcelain modeler, was not a potter but a goldsmith.
The pots and containers were comparatively clumsy with sharp contours and they
had to be finished and decorated after the burning process (Figs. 1, 2, 3 and 4).

With repeated experiments and hard work the porcelain paste and especially
the glaze were improved. When the artists became more familiar with porcelain,
they soon realized that it was the ideal plastic material which could be formed and
decorated into most interesting and artistic objects. The copying of metal wares
was largely abandoned and forms and decorations of East Asiatic porcelain were
adopted. Painting of porcelain came into fashion, and Chinese and Japanese scenes
of life and landscapes dominated for a while (Figs. 5, 6, 7 and 8).

The styles or fashions of porcelain modeling and decorating were naturally
influenced by contemporary artistic and architectural styles. Porcelain fashions

generally changed with the artistic trends, although there was considerable lagging and overlapping of the different styles. In some regions and among some factories the prevailing fashions emerged earlier than in others.

Realizing that it is impossible to ascribe a definite period to a specific style and vice versa, the following succession of porcelain fashions generally prevailed during the 18th and 19th centuries:

The *Baroque* style prevailed when MEISSEN discovered porcelain, and continued in fashion during its first years of operation. Baroque is characterized by its massive form, great contrast of light and shadows and vigorous action. The plastic modeling and ornamental painting were combined into an entity. Strong and bright surface colors enriched the vivid naturalistic figures, the heavily ornamented tableware and other objects. Typical examples of the Baroque motif are shown in Figures 16, 18, 31, 52 and 87.

The *Regence* style, so called after the regency of Philip of Orleans who ruled France after the death of Louis XIV until Louis XV became of age, appeared in porcelain forms and decorations around 1725 and largely replaced the Baroque. It is not just a transition between the Baroque and Rococo although it possesses features of both. The Regence style turns from the heavy pompous motif of Louis XIV to more delicate designs characterized by curved lines, scrolls and leaves and a light, unrestrained air.

The influence of the *Rococo* style which evolved from the Baroque and Regence first appeared in porcelain around 1735, became prominent in 1750 to 1755, and remained in vogue until about 1770 to 1780. The Rococo fashion is characterized by its light graceful design, its fanciful forms and succession of curved lines and scrolls. The pieces of this period are decorated with trifling ornaments symbolic of the elite, carefree, pleasure-seeking peoples of that time. Characteristics of the Baroque continue into the Rococo period, but they take on a more graceful and delicate form with many C- and S-curves. Heavy buds now develop into light flowers. Fruit and flowers are strewn all over the surface of the subject in a gay and charming manner. Little figures and cupids play between bushes and *rocailles* on mirror frames, clocks and chandeliers. Harmonious light and delicate colors are employed in a most pleasing manner. Characteristic examples of the Rococo style are shown in Figures 35, 36, 37, 41, 71, 81, 96, 104, 116, 132 and 144.

The art of porcelain reached its zenith toward the end of the Rococo period. Modelers and painters had found porcelain to be the ideal medium for materializing their conception of both form and color, and lavished their talents on this unusual substance. On no other material could the colors of Baroque and Rococo be more permanently portrayed, as paintings on canvas, wood and other materials change with age. On porcelain, paintings are fused in the glass through the glazing and firing process and retain their original colors indefinitely.

It is particularly interesting to note that the most artistic porcelain was produced in Germany during the lifetime of August the Strong of Saxony (1670-1733), George II of England (1683-1760), and Louis XV of France (1710-1774). The art reached its height and began to decline before Maria Theresa, Empress of Austria (1717-1780), and Frederick the Great, King of Prussia (1712-1786) had died; a few years before George Washington (1732-1799) became the first President of the United States (1789); and almost a half century before Napoleon (1769-1821) ruled as Emperor (1804-1814).

With the social and economic changes which took place after the middle of the 18th century and with the development of the natural sciences during the last third of the same century, court tradition and fantasy began to fade. The trend was toward a simple and natural way of life. Consequently, from 1760 to 1770 the so-called *Louis Seize* style developed in France and spread to Germany and other European countries, reaching its climax during the reign of Louis XVI (1774-1793). The *Louis Seize* fashion (Figs. 43 and 135), forerunner of the stronger *Classical* development, generally occupied designers in the last part of the 18th century. Outstanding articles of porcelain were produced at some of the German factories during the *Louis Seize* period especially at MEISSEN, VIENNA and BERLIN.

The German artists who were responsible for the creation of the Baroque style and willingly accepted the French Rococo features were reluctant to adopt the simpler *Neo-Classical* innovations which tended toward the elimination of fanciful designs and colors. They insisted on clinging to the established light touch of color and charm and consequently lost the leadership in porcelain art to SEVRES. Honey states, "Eventually, however, a desire to emulate the Classical marble made the unglazed, unpainted 'biscuit' porcelain the universal medium, and in striving after the monumental, the modelers abandoned all that was distinctive and valuable in porcelain. The same loss of porcelain-sense was shown in the practice of completely covering up the surface of the beautiful white material with pictorial miniature paintings. 'Truth of Nature' was once more the battle-cry among the painters; but here it denied the convention that made the art of porcelain possible. Thus it was only when porcelain had become familiar and its artistic possibilities were for the time exhausted that porcelain painting and modeling lost the living, sensitive and exciting touch that entitled them to the name of creative art."

The spirit of quiet Classical forms continued to develop as the result of the great excavations of Pompeii and Herculaneum and other prevailing influences. The shell adornments gradually disappeared, being replaced by beads, wreaths adorned with ribbons, torches, darts and shields. Ornaments became more and more independent of the body with which it formed an entity during the Baroque and Rococo periods, and straight lines largely replaced the former curved contours. Little remained of the gay Rococo colors. The unpainted biscuit porcelain which was unglazed tried to imitate the cool marble sculpture of the Classical times. The handles of vases, pots and cups, and the spouts of coffee- and tea-pots became less curved and more angular. The curved brims and *rocaille* handles of trays and bowls were replaced with rectangles and straight lines, and symmetry dominated the general pattern, as shown in Figures 79, 94, 107, 142, 146 and 168.

Associated with the increasing classical trend instigated by SEVRES, Claissicism evolved during the last part of the 18th century and prevailed beyond Napoleon's reign, 1804 to 1814, during which time it was referred to as the *Empire* style. The light touch and charm of Rococo form and colors had almost disappeared, and the pompous military influences dominated the Empire period. Straight lines and an air of symmetry prevailed as the Egyptian, Greek and Roman influences came into prominence. Sphinx-like ornaments were used as handles or feet on vases and vase lids. Greek and Roman portraits and silhouettes appeared in reserved panel paintings, and realistic town and countryside panoramas replaced the fantastic landscapes of the Rococo period. Representative specimens of the Empire motif are shown in Figures 61 and 65.

The Empire style was translated into the *Biedermeier*, a typical German fashion, from about 1820 to 1845. The Biedermeier typifies the comparatively simple manner of the middle-class peoples, the *bourgeois*, who had gained recognition in the social structure during this time. Some characteristics of the Empire period were carried over into the Biedermeier, but there was a strong tendency to make quite plain well-proportioned services and other items with limited and simple decorations. Flowers were depicted growing naturally out of the earth and scenes typifying the modest way of life predominated (Figs. 99 and 122).

After the Biedermeier period, long years followed without a typical style for porcelain. The period beginning around 1840 was greatly influenced by the technical sciences of the industrial age. Some old styles were revived and new creations attempted, but artistic developments floundered without any great contributions. The so-called "Youth style," *Jugendstil*, generally given the French designation, *Style nouveau*, came into fashion around 1900. This was followed by what is referred to as the modern style, *Moderner Stil*, in which traces of the Rococo fashion reappear (Figs. 48 and 49).

The factories made repeated attempts to improve their styles and production techniques, but it was not until the beginning of the 20th century that creative progress was renewed in the porcelain industry. COPENHAGEN, for example, developed an underglaze high-temperature coloring which opened new possibilities. Various factories introduced technical and artistic innovations, along with their good and bad features, which gave new impulses to the industry. These developments will be discussed under the factories in Chapters III and IV.

COLLECTORS AND COLLECTIONS

Porcelain collecting dates back to the Turkish Sultans who had made famous acquisitions as early as the 15th century. Their great passion is shown by large collections in the old Serail and the Museum of Constantinople which contain about 10,000 pieces of porcelain. Selim I (1467-1520) acquired the first pieces for these assemblages but his son and successor, Soliman the Magnificent (1495-1566), added many pieces to these collections, which contain Chinese porcelain dating from the Sung Dynasty (960-1279) to the 18th century. It is believed that many of these pieces were captured from the Persians by the Turkish Sultans and brought to Constantinople.

The first Western European porcelain collectors were Louis XIV (1638-1715) and the Dauphin and the Duchess of Orleans. Louis XIV, the Sun King, erected the Trianon of Porcelain in the Park of Versailles and dedicated it to his mistress, the Marquise de Montespan, as a tea-house. This tea-house which no longer exists introduced the vogue of porcelain cabinets or galleries to the European Courts. The idea of absolutism had developed around the courts, and the showing of magnificence was a sign of power. Consequently, the porcelain displays served as princely show windows from about 1675 to 1750.

August the Strong was the first famous German porcelain collector. He had an unrestrained love for oriental porcelain and his East Asia collection was incomparable in value and extent. Many stories were told about his indulgence in acquiring porcelain. One related that he traded 12 "big men" from his personal guard to the King of Prussia for 48 beautiful porcelain vases which were jokingly referred to as "soldier vases," *Dragonervasen*. It is not difficult, therefore, to understand that under the influence of such an ardent admirer and connoisseur, hard-paste porcelain was first made in Europe in one of his castles in Meissen.

Porcelain Cabinet in the Castle of Charlottenburg, about 1705, by Eosander von Göthe.

As the porcelain frenzy spread, famous cabinets and galleries of the valued ceramics were established in the Castles of Charlottenburg, Oranienburg and Ansbach; in the Dubsky Palais, Brünn; in Vienna, and in other localities throughout Europe during the 18th century. In addition many of the smaller princes and aristocrats made notable collections of Chinese, German, French and other porcelains. These outstanding porcelain displays were arranged symmetrically on gilded consoles, aiming at decorative impressions in the taste of Baroque. The porcelain pieces were displayed to give a mass exhibition rather than individual impressions.

The fever of porcelain collecting subsided between 1760 and 1780, but a new era opened for porcelain amateurs and collectors with the establishment of the large German museums during the last half of the 19th century. Extensive public collections were assembled in museums of the principal cities of Germany including the Museums of Art and Craft in Berlin, Frankfurt, Dresden, Hamburg, Munich, Cologne and in a number of province museums.

In addition to the museum collections, numerous well-to-do German bankers, industrialists and merchants became interested in porcelain and made outstanding accumulations. The Rothschilds of Frankfurt and Vienna were great collectors of 18th century porcelain, and old porcelain was acquired by numerous noble as well as *bourgeois* families and handed down from one generation to another. The most notable private collection was that of Hermine Feist of Berlin. It contained many of the most valuable pieces of the 18th century and was acquired by the Schlossmuseum of Berlin in 1935. Most of the other outstanding private collections have been dispersed over the world in years past, and only the illustrated auction catalogs of the large German auction firms remain to show their size and quality and indicate the zeal of the porcelain collectors at that time. Since these catalogs were prepared with great care by art historians, they serve as excellent reference sources for the amateur and dealer. The principal catalogs are listed by name, address, and date of publication in the Appendix on page 226.

In similar fashion, museums and private collectors of other countries, including America, made distinguished collections of old porcelains. American interest in European and Continental porcelain has greatly increased during the 20th century, especially after World Wars I and II. Many pieces and collections of first rank have been acquired from Germany, England, France and elsewhere. Porcelain admirers and amateur collectors in the United States are now counted in the thousands. Some of the more serious connoisseurs have outstanding collections. For example, Mr. and Mrs. G. Ryland Scott and Mr. and Mrs. Charles B. Stout exhibited their large collections of excellent quality 18th century Continental and English porcelains jointly and independently in the Brooks Memorial Art Gallery in Memphis in 1955 and again in 1956. Their individual collections, which have resulted from international searchings for several years, have attracted widespread attention and typify the growing interest in various sections of the United States. Liberal bequests have also been made by individuals and estates to museums and other institutions. To give only one example, the J. P. Morgan Collection which was presented to the Wadsworth Atheneum of Hartford, contains 360 old MEISSEN figures and groups alone.

Frequent porcelain exhibitions are held by museums, commercial galleries and individuals in various parts of the country. Some are confined to porcelain of a certain country or style, while others include variety to stress general qualities of a certain period. For instance the Metropolitan Museum of Art in New York displayed in 1949 about 500 figures, groups and other 18th century items of porcelain from 26 old European factories. Eight prominent private collectors and four museums provided pieces for the exhibition. Although no attempt was made to represent all European countries or indicate the relative importance of porcelain of different sources, it is interesting to note that of the 546 pieces described in the exhibition catalog, 215 were of German manufacture, 177 English, 102 French, 24 Austrian, 24 Italian, and 4 were Spanish.

INFLUENCE OF WORLD WAR II

As previously indicated, large quantities of German and Austrian porcelain were acquired by Americans and other nationals preceding World War II; however, many collections remained. The extent of war loss and damage to private and public German collections is of universal concern, but can never be accurately ascertained. However, it is known that a number of the private collections were partially or completely destroyed, misplaced, sold, or otherwise dispersed during

27

and following hostilities. For example, the famous collections of von Dallwitz of Berlin and Erich Wolf of Guben, Mark Brandenburg, were extinguished during the war. Some museums suffered loss and damage to their porcelain and other items as a direct result of the war or through breakage in handling or storage, while others may never be able to retrieve their original possessions which were stored in certain areas of Germany.

Cautious German collectors and most museums moved their art treasures from the cities to places of safe keeping preceding and during hostilities. Since most of the museums, a large per cent of the residences of private collectors and some of the castles which treasured porcelain were destroyed or damaged, a considerable quantity of valuable items necessarily remained in storage until adequate space was provided for redisplaying. However, practically all of the museums in Western Germany reopened in their original or improvised buildings within two or three years after the cessation of hostilities, and those which could find adequate space revived their porcelain exhibitions soon thereafter. Ten years after the War most of the museums of Western Germany were displaying their former porcelain treasures with some modifications.

German museums and private connoisseurs attach much sentiment and material value to their art treasures and are inclined to retain their best pieces under any circumstances. Although considerable quantities of porcelain of commercial or semi-artistic grade were damaged, destroyed or bartered during the turbulent war years, it is reasonable to assume that a very high percentage of the prewar artistic porcelain was saved in Western Germany.

The growing fondness in America for European porcelain, which is attested by the large number of collections acquired in recent years, is expected to continue. This interest was greatly stimulated following World War II when thousands of military and civilian personnel and tourists gained an appreciation of high quality German porcelain. Many acquired good pieces along with the inferior items which were so plentiful. Indications are that amateurs will continue to accumulate artistic porcelain with increasing enthusiasm and appreciation. They have found in the hobby of collecting a most satisfying way of enjoying leisure, and a secret of enriching their lives.

CHAPTER II

The Production of Porcelain

The first European porcelain was produced under closely-guarded conditions, shrouded in mystery; however, during the last part of the 18th century most of the methods of production became generally known. Despite the fact that the factories tried to protect their secrets, Franz Joseph Weber published a book in 1798 entitled *"Die Kunst das ächte Porzellain zu verfertigen"* in which he explained porcelain production and gave other interesting and historical facts on the old factories. Much was written on this subject later, but the most scientific information was provided by Hermann August **Seger**, a German scientist who dedicated himself to the study of ceramics in several European countries. After holding a number of important positions, he became chief of the chemical-technical research department of the BERLIN Porcelain Manufactory in 1878. He established a series of standard porcelain formulae known as the "Seger Formulae" and is responsible for the "Seger Cones" which are used to determine the fusing temperature of various ceramic mixtures. He wrote voluminously on his findings, primarily during the last quarter of the 19th century, and his complete works are now combined in *"Seger's Gesammelte Schriften."*

Although porcelain production is no longer a mystery, many modern factories claim to have special and improved formulae for making paste and glaze mixtures and for modeling and firing their products, which they carefully preserve. Continuous research is being done by individual factories and publicly supported research institutions to improve the quality and production methods of porcelain and to train technicians and artists. The most important German institution of this kind is the State Technical Porcelain Institute, *Meisterschule für Porzellan, Staatliche Fachschule*, at Selb, Bavaria.

The composition and production methods of hard-paste German porcelain may vary somewhat among factories, but the basic procedures are practically the same now as in the past. The process of manufacturing porcelain is divided into several parts, namely: (1) preparing raw materials; (2) shaping or molding; (3) firing, glazing and refiring; and (4) decorating or painting. The composition and production of porcelain is briefly explained in the following sections, and its relationship to other ceramics is graphically illustrated on page 38 and described in the Glossary.

PREPARING RAW MATERIALS

Porcelain is made from a mixture of about 50 per cent kaolin (a porcelain clay composed of silicate of aluminium which is difficult to fuse) and approximately 25 per cent quartz, and 25 per cent feldspar which under high temperature forms a fusible glass and acts as a flux. The relative amounts of the three ingredients vary according to the texture desired — the more kaolin the harder the porcelain. The ingredients are carefully washed, ground and pulverized before they are mixed together as a paste. The water is pressed out of the creamy mass, forming plastic cakes which were formerly stored for 12 to 14 months in cellars of low temperature and proper humidity but are now stored for shorter periods. The cakes when properly aged are thrown into a mixing machine which produces a consistent dough for modeling or turning.

SHAPING OR MOLDING

Porcelain pieces are shaped by turning, molding or casting and by embossing. All articles such as plates, bowls, vases and cups which have a cylindrical shape, are usually turned on the potter's wheel and formed with the hands and with mechanical aids (Fig. A). For flat articles such as plates and saucers, gypsum molds are used for the inside or concave part. The lower part of the flat piece which is

PRODUCTION OF PORCELAIN

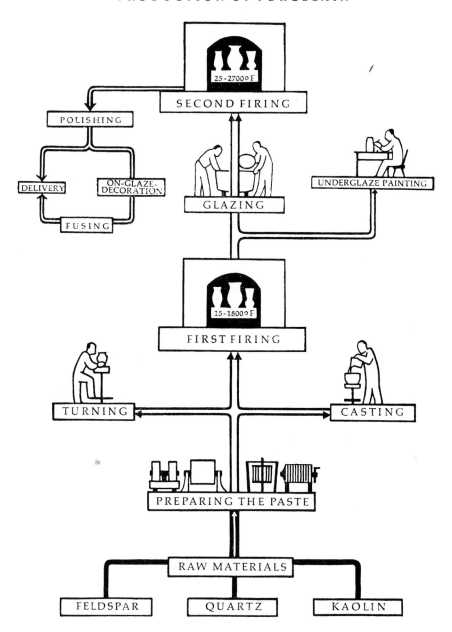

SECOND FIRING
25-2700° F

POLISHING

DELIVERY

ON-GLAZE-DECORATION

FUSING

GLAZING

UNDERGLAZE PAINTING

FIRST FIRING
15-1800° F

TURNING

CASTING

PREPARING THE PASTE

RAW MATERIALS

FELDSPAR   QUARTZ   KAOLIN

Prepared by the State Technical Porcelain Institute, Selb

Fig. A "Thrower" at the Potter's Wheel with Mechanical Forming Aid

turned bottom-side-up in the turning process is shaped by means of a pattern of metal which is pressed against the rotating mass until the superfluous paste is removed and the desired thickness attained.

Molds are also used to produce items of the same size and shape such as figures, non-cylindrical cups and candlesticks. The molds are composed of a gypsum material (plaster of Paris) which absorbs the water contained in the porcelain paste in a short time, thereby permitting the piece under formation to shrink away from the molds without changing in shape. For hollow globe- or bulb-shaped wares, such as tea-pots and odd-shaped vases, a two-piece plaster mold is used to form the outside pattern. The mold is poured completely full of the liquid porcelain paste from which water is absorbed, allowing the paste to harden next to the walls of the molds. Within a few minutes, when the proper thickness of paste adheres to the mold, the remaining fluid paste in the interior is poured out. After slight drying the two parts of the mold are removed, the fresh piece is checked for defects, and after drying sufficiently, it is ready for firing.

Fig. B   "Repairers" Joining the Pieces of Figures

To make figures, groups and unusual objects, the model is divided into several parts from which two-piece molds are made for each part. The same raw porcelain material is used, but it is more liquid in consistency and can be poured readily into the mold. After drying, the repairer or embosser takes the various parts from the molds and joins them together with a thin slip paste. It is then the difficult task of the repairer to remove the surplus slip from the connected pieces, smooth the seams and refine the piece (Fig. B). In making modern lacy-dress figures, real lace is dipped into a thin porcelain paste or slip. The lace is then draped by hand on the plastic figure until the desired fashion is attained. In the firing process the fiber of the lace disintegrates leaving a pattern of hard porcelain material in its place.

The handles, most other projecting parts, plastic ornaments and reliefs of table-ware and other objects are also molded. They are then embossed or attached to the main piece in the same manner as assembling the pieces of a figure. When the objects is finally formed from the raw material either by turning, molding, casting, embossing, impressing or engraving, it is carefully dried and then fired.

Fig. C   Placing Pieces in Saggers Before Firing

FIRING AND GLAZING

Under high temperature the raw porcelain object undergoes a thorough chemical change in the kiln and shrinks about 16 per cent in height and 14 per cent in thickness or diameter. The kaolin combines with the fusible ingredients of quartz and feldspar, and the physical properties of the new mass emerge with materially different physical characteristics from those of the raw materials.

Porcelain is fired two, three or more times according to the quality and degree of painting and gilding desired. In the production of ordinary porcelain, the first or "glow burning" is made at about 1500 to 1800° F (800 to 1000° C) to eliminate all moisture and harden it sufficiently for handling. In this state porcelain is commonly referred to as "glowpaste," is brittle and porous and absorbs the fluid glaze freely. The piece is then hand dipped into the liquid glaze which is approximately the same material as that for making porcelain except that more feldspar and other fluxes have been added to promote fusion. In the dipping process, the piece is uniformly

Fig. D Painters Applying Decorations

covered with a thin layer of the fluid-glaze material. The water in the glaze is soon absorbed by the dry porous piece which then takes on a powdered appearance. Following the glazing the second or "sharp" firing is made at the high temperature of 2550 to 2650° F (1400 to 1450° C), and the porcelain attains its distinctive and final state. The resulting product is genuine porcelain, the highest grade product in the field of ceramics. It is the hard, white, fine-textured, translucent, acid-resistant, impervious, low-heat-conducting, resonant material which lends itself to so many artistic and utilitarian purposes.

During the firing the porcelain pieces are placed in fire-clay boxes, called "saggers," to afford protection against flaky ashes and flames and to facilitate proper stacking in the kilns (Fig. C). One or more pieces can be placed in each sagger, depending upon the sizes. Since saggers can be used only a few times, and so much additional space is required by them, their use necessarily increases the cost of the production considerably. The refiring, after decoration, is discussed in the following section.

DECORATING

Figures and other pieces of painted porcelain received their finishing touches or artistic completion in the decorating rooms. Able artists made designs from a large variety of pictures and natural scenes and adapted them to porcelain objects of all kinds. The painters, especially those in early times, had a very sensitive feeling toward their porcelain subjects. Each piece was decorated individually and no two were painted alike. This is particularly true of the early 18th century figures, many of which appear as living characters. Even today the old factories of MEISSEN, NYMPHENBURG and BERLIN paint all of their pieces by hand. However, it has become common practice for individual painters to apply specific colors or subjects on similar pieces in assembly-line fashion (Fig. D). Consequently, the best modern decorations lack the vivid touch which was associated with the masters of the 18th century. Most modern factories decorate their pieces mechanically by steel-plate or chromatic printings.

In general there are two ways of decorating porcelain. The first method applies the plastic decorations on the rough unfired body of the piece itself in the form of reliefs, perforations, embossings, or simply by impressing or engraving. This may be called "decoration in the white" since all of these additions are made on the original soft mass. Various factories have developed special patterns in relief. For example, the *Ozier* (Figs. 40 and 41), *Flechtmuster* and *Marseillezierat* were developed by MEISSEN while *Englischglatt* and *Reliefzierat mit Spalier* are creations of BERLIN.

The second method of decoration is accomplished by coloring or gilding. Colored metallic oxides are used and the colors are applied either "under the glaze" after the first firing or "on the glaze" following the second firing. The palette of on-glaze colors is rich and varied, while the technical difficulties of underglaze painting limit the color range considerably. The special underglaze colors which can stand the high temperature of the second or "sharp" firing are usually applied on the once-fired "glowpaste" porcelain before glazing. The piece is then glazed which partially obscures the painting, but the "sharp" firing vitrifies the glaze and the decoration reappears. The enamel colors which are prepared with oil and turpentine and the gold decorations are applied on the glaze after the high-temperature

36

firing. When paintings are applied on the glaze, it is necessary to fire the pieces for the third time in a muffle oven at about 1300 to 1450° F (800 to 900° C). This allows the enamel colors to be fused on the glaze and durably united with it. Gold decorations are the last to be applied and are fixed by a special burning.

Many modern factories decorate most of their utilitarian porcelain by ceramic decalcomanias or transfers. The desired designs in various colors including gold are printed on glassene paper and transferred directly to the object which is later fired at approximately 1250° F.

The procedure described is not always so simple. Richly decorated porcelain may in some instances be fired as many as four or even five times according to the kinds of paints and gildings applied. For example, when the decoration of a piece includes both cobalt and gold, it passes through a "glow burning," a "smooth burning," a special "cobalt sharp burning" at about 1600° F (1000° C), and one or two "gold burnings." In any event, after the final firing, the decorations are polished and the complicated procedure of manufacturing the piece is completed.

Not all porcelain, however, is glazed and decorated. Large quantities of marble-white porcelain, so-called "biscuit," have been produced, especially during the Neo-Classical and Empire periods from about 1780 to 1820. The ingredients of "biscuit" are ground to a finer texture and more feldspar is added than in ordinary porcelain. The special paste is usually fired twice, the "glow burning" and then a "smooth burning" without glaze, but biscuit can be produced by one smooth burning. The resulting biscuit porcelain is a beautiful smooth marble-like product which some people prefer to glazed porcelain (Figs. 100, 101 and 111).

CRAFTSMANSHIP

As can be seen, the various phases of porcelain production require more skill, exactness, care and personal interest than almost any other kind of manufacturing. The chemists, modelers, designers, painters and skilled technicians are thoroughly trained in the basic principles of the craft in highly specialized vocational schools, and are then required to serve several years as apprentices under master supervision. Frequently whole families are engaged in the industry over generations.

Factories place a high premium on expert workmanship as mistakes in any stage of production result in defective pieces and unnecessary expence. All workers play an important, inseparable role. The chemists and technicians are responsible for seeing that the right blend, color, and texture of paste and glaze are mixed for the various requirements. The chief modeler and his staff of artists must necessarily use great skill and good taste in designing and modeling objects which will create and perpetuate a demand. The throwers and molders have the responsibility of fashioning the items according to definite specifications, while the painstaking duty of the embosser or repairer is to assemble and join the molded pieces expertly with a slip paste. No less important is the responsibility of the kiln-master and his careful attendants who are required to know exactly at what temperature and how long the pieces are to be fired and cooled. Then come the important decorators to make the finishing touches by applying various ornaments, combinations of colors, designs under and on the glaze and by adding gold trimmings.

In all, a well-organized highly-trained group of artists and craftsmen are necessary to produce high quality porcelain — men and women who love their work and feel that they are playing the most important role in producing an object of beauty and utility.

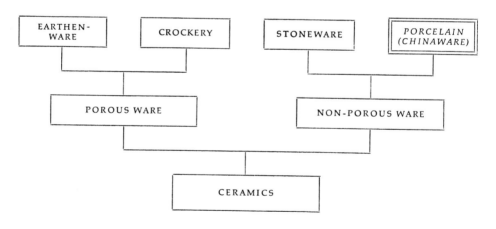

BRANCHES OF CERAMICS

Prepared by The State Technical Porcelain Institute, Selb

CHAPTER III

Major Porcelain Factories

The great variety of artistic porcelain produced by the early German manufactories was generally lavish, highly decorative and animated; but there were noticeable differences in the style, paste, form and decoration of the various enterprises. The cultural life of France was concentrated around one court, while in Germany there were many small courts which, as cultural centers, competed with one another. This fact explains the great variety of German porcelain which was produced by the several royal and princely porcelain establishments. Honey states, "Though the same types of ware were made by all, each of the major factories achieved an individual style. There was in Germany no royal monopoly like that in France protecting the SEVRES establishment to prevent the rise of more than one factory and free play was given to variety in taste and patronage."

The factories as individual institutions are of considerable interest to amateurs and collectors. Therefore, the history, quality of materials, principal personalities, the styles, the specialities of production, and the marks of the eight major German and Austrian factories will be discussed in this chapter. They include MEISSEN, VIENNA, HÖCHST, FÜRSTENBERG, NYMPHENBURG, BERLIN, FRANKENTHAL, and LUDWIGSBURG, listed in chronological order of their establishment. In addition, one section is devoted to the independent decorators, *Hausmaler*, who were so active in Germany and other parts of Europe primarily in the second quarter of the 18th century. The geographical locations of the German and other European porcelain factories which started operating in the 18th century are shown on the map, page 41.

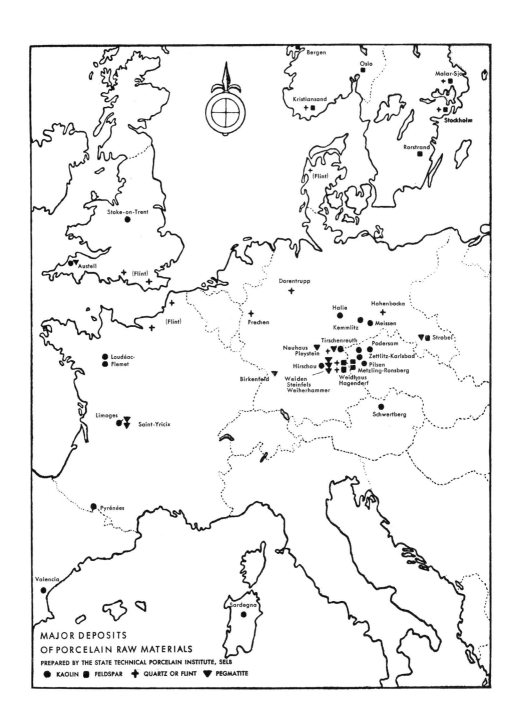

MAJOR DEPOSITS
OF PORCELAIN RAW MATERIALS

PREPARED BY THE STATE TECHNICAL PORCELAIN INSTITUTE, SELB

● KAOLIN ■ FELDSPAR ✚ QUARTZ OR FLINT ▼ PEGMATITE

40

Marieberg

Liverpool
Spode
Minton   Pinxton
Longport   Derby
Worcester
Swansea
Bristol   Bow
Chelsea
Lowestoft

Copenhagen

Haag
Weesp
Berlin

Bruxelles
Fürstenberg
Kassel   Tomaszow
Lille   Tournay
Gotha   Volkstedt   Meissen
Rouen   Arras   Höchst   Fulda   Gera
Caen   Ilmenau   Limbach   Proszowice
St. Cloud   Kelsterbach   Kloster Veilsdorf
Paris   Ottweiler   Wallendorf   Klösterle
Sèvres   Würzburg   Prag
Niederweiler   Frankenthal   Schlaggenwald
Orleans   Gutenbrunn   Ansbach
Strassburg
Ludwigsburg
Limoges   Nymphenburg   Wien
Nyon   Zürich   (Vienna)
Bordeaux

Nove
Treviso
Vinovo
Venezia
Este
Marseille

Gerona

Napoli
(Naples)

THE 18TH CENTURY
EUROPEAN PORCELAIN FACTORIES

BOUNDARIES AS OF 1933

■ MAJOR GERMAN FACTORIES   ▲ OTHER GERMAN FACTORIES   ● NON-GERMAN FACTORIES

41

MEISSEN
(1710 to Present Date)

The MEISSEN factory was established in Meissen, 14 miles from Dresden, in 1710 by the great porcelain enthusiast and collector August the Strong soon after the German discovery of true porcelain by Johann Friedrich Böttger (Page 16). In every way MEISSEN is considered the foremost German factory — first to be founded, leader in the creation of form and decoration in Europe until about 1756, and generally successful in its long and continuous operations.

The first period of MEISSEN, from 1710 to 1719, is referred to as the "Böttger Period." Likewise, later "Periods" of the factory are associated with the names of notables or events. Böttger, who served as director of the factory from its beginning, was a frail temperamental alchemist with little talent for business or art. He was confronted with many difficulties, but was fortunate in securing the services of a number of competent specialists on his staff. They included Samuel Stöltzel as manager of the paste and kilns; Johann J. Irminger and Georg Fritzsche, modelers; Konrad Christoph Hunger and Cornelius Funk, gold decorators; and David Köhler as underglaze decorator.

Böttger favored his original reddish brown stoneware, *Böttger Steinzeug*, and considered his creation a ceramic marvel (Fig. 1). It is the hardest stoneware of the period, and it can be cut only with an emery wheel or a diamond. It lends itself to a beautiful polish and is occasionally painted with lacquer (Fig. 2). Pieces were modeled from original oriental objects or fashioned after silver and metal containers as no special style had been established for this material (Figs. 1 and 2). During the first years of MEISSEN's operation, Böttger produced a whitish soft-tone, creamy-yellow appearing paste, known as *Böttger Porzellan*. This was the first hard-paste porcelain produced in Europe and some pieces were fashioned after Chinese and Japanese originals while others were decorated in relief with birds, vines, and fruits like contemporary silverwares (Fig. 3). Various small objects were made including pots, vases, trays and unusual figures (Fig. 4).

The factory never reached a successful state of production under Böttger's brief direction as he was plagued with financial and general managerial as well as personnel problems. Broken in spirit and health and addicted to drink, Böttger who

42

had made the great discovery, died in 1719 at the early age of 37. Despite his frailties he is regarded as the genius who made possible one of the greatest artistic products of the 18th century. His contribution brought about the Baroque MEISSEN of Höroldt and Kändler which has enriched the world.

During Böttger's time the porcelain paste was of a slight greyish or yellow tint. Although it was not always consistent in composition or highly translucent, it had a slightly yellow tone without spots or tares when viewed by transmitted light. In order to produce a more desirable white medium upon which to portray beautiful paintings, a small amount of cobalt blue was added to the porcelain mixture beginning about 1720. The blue combined with the increased amount of iron oxide in the paste produced a pure white material. This combination gave the porcelain a greenish color associated with thin or more translucent spots of variable sizes and shapes when viewed by transmitted light. These spots, referred to as "moons" or "tares", were prevalent in most of MEISSEN's products from 1720, with decreasing conspicuousness, to about 1750 or even later. In recent years, collectors are learning to associate the "moons" and green color with the old porcelain of the period described.

Through constant experimentation, the paste was brought to a pure hard white consistency, the translucency was increased and a porcelain of uniform white quality was developed somewhere around 1750. The glaze which was at first comparatively thick was made thinner, and more brilliant.

August the Strong became more active in the factory after Böttger died. MEISSEN was reorganized and placed on a more functional working basis by 1720. Fortunately, Johann Gregor Höroldt (1696-1775), a former color chemist of the newly-established VIENNA factory, was made responsible for MEISSEN's operation in 1720. The young Höroldt made such a favorable impression on the Saxon authorities that in 1723 he was appointed court painter, *Hofmaler*. His work was so outstanding that he became director in 1731 with the title of royal commissioner, *Hofkommissar*. He wisely retained the able assistants of Böttger, secured or trained other artists and craftsmen and developed the MEISSEN organization into one of high morale and efficiency. Improved quality and increased production were soon reflected in the factory's financial success. The period from 1720 to 1731 is appropriately referred to as the "Höroldt Period."

Höroldt, who frequently employed the Regence style, first copied the Far Eastern Indian flowers, *Indianische Blumen*, and the bamboo and cherry blossoms and hedge paintings of Japanese Imari porcelain. Dragon and fantastic bird decorations from Chinese porcelain were also employed. A few of his earliest pieces were European and Asiatic scenes decorated in gold. He and Cornelius Funk, an understudy gilder created some beautiful monotone golden scenes which are similar to and often confused with Augsburg *Hausmalerei* decorations (Figs. 5 and 6). Beginning around 1725, Höroldt instituted the famous brilliant multicolored Chinese paintings known as *chinoiseries*. They vividly portray the mythical carefree existence of Far Eastern peoples in intricate gold or lustre frames (Figs. 7 and 8). The European vogue for *chinoiseries* nowhere found better expression than by Höroldt and his associates who applied them on numerous pieces no two of which are alike. By 1730 the market was almost saturated with *chinoiseries*, but they were painted in reduced numbers for another ten years.

A group of unusual vases made only for August the Strong and marked AR, for Augustus Rex, in underglaze blue are very rare but frequently copied (Marks 1 and 9, pages 106 and 110, respectively). The vases were designed after Chinese models but are more exaggerated in color and general features (Colored Plate I).

Between 1730 and 1740 Höroldt, with his cousin Christian Friedrich Herold, the brilliant young painter Adam Friedrich von Löwenfink, Johann Georg Heintze and other associates reached the zenith of their art. In addition to the *chinoiseries*, decorations in Japanese *Kakiemon* or *Makiemon* patterns were applied sparsely on individual pieces and services. Their drawings also depicted gardens, hunting scenes, boats and harbors and landscape in beautiful Baroque frames of lattice and scrolls (Fig. 9), and Löwenfink is especially famous for his fantastic fable animal paintings (Fig. 10). During this period Höroldt and his associates also copied the Chinese flower designs from pieces of the royal collection, and produced what is known as the highly decorative "oriental flowers," *Indianische Blumen*, on flat surfaces or in relief (Fig. 32). They also designed the so-called European or German flowers, *Deutsche Blumen* (Figs. 33, 34, and 41), from colored engravings; and by 1740 they were making charming paintings from real flowers (Fig. 45). Höroldt, being a painter, placed more emphasis on decoration than on modeling which he tended to neglect. He was soon forced to realize, however, that surface

Plate I "Augustus Rex" Vase with Yellow Ground and Fabulous Animals.
About 1730 (Page 44).   *Bayerisches Nationalmuseum, Munich*

MEISSEN

decoration was only one part of the product, so he decided to improve the styles and methods of modeling. In 1727, Johann Gottlob Kirchner was engaged and proved an able modeler of figures, animals, clocks, vases and elaborate pieces for table decorations but was released because of his unreliability. His successor Johann Christian Ludwig von Lücke also proved unsatisfactory, and it was not until 1731 when the 25-year-old court sculptor Johann Joachim Kändler (1706-1775) was engaged that the problem of modeling was solved. Kändler adapted the late Baroque style to porcelain and improved the whole modeling department. Consequently the modeling of MEISSEN became outstanding soon after his arrival. He proved to be a master and a living inspiration to the porcelain artists throughout Europe. Kändler is generally recognized as the greatest modeler of porcelain with the possible exception of Franz Anton Bustelli of NYMPHENBURG, who is believed by some to have equalled or even excelled Kändler in the fashioning of figures and groups (Page 61).

For the most part MEISSEN produced small tea and coffee services and individual items before the arrival of Kändler, but under his influence the scope of operations was materially increased. It was not until his genius was joined with that of Höroldt that MEISSEN porcelain attained its maximum variety, grace and beauty and reached the peak of its fame around 1750. These two great artists enjoyed a long successful career together, and the period from 1731 to 1756, the beginning of the Seven Years War, is known as the "Höroldt-Kändler Period."

August the Strong died in 1733 and was succeeded by his son, August III. The new Prime Minister Count Heinrich von Brühl was appointed director of the factory, in which position he proved to be very successful. Höroldt continued as manager and chief artist, and Kändler produced his wonderful conceptions of plastic art — full of life, grace and charm. His creations included a great variety of items of all sizes — figures, services, candelabra, desk sets, and life-like birds and animals and many kinds of vases (Fig. 11).

The new King, August III, and director Brühl enjoyed the privilege of obtaining porcelain without charge from the royal factory. They vied with each other by ordering unusual pieces of porcelain and special dinner services for their friends, and Kändler and Höroldt cooperated generously in that it gave them an opportunity to display their genius. Several famous services were produced before and soon after Kändler arrived—the "Yellow Tiger" service, about 1728, being perhaps the earliest (Fig. 12); followed by the "Red Dragon," about 1730 (Fig. 13); and a service with the Saxonian-Polish coat of arms was produced about 1733 (Fig. 14). Between 1735 and 1737 Kändler executed his Baroque genius fully on the famous Sulkowski service for the Saxonian-Polish Minister, Count Sulkowski (Figs. 15 and 16). His greatest achievement, however, was the production of the magnificent "Swan Service" for Count Brühl. The Swan Service is reputed to be the most important and most interesting ever made. Kändler, with the help of his right-hand man Johann Friedrich Eberlein and a number of assistants, was engaged from 1737 to 1741 on the 1400 – piece set which was made for and bears the coat of arms of Count Brühl and his wife Countess Antonie von Kollowrat. As the name suggests, swans are shown in relief or in-the-round on the various pieces in Baroque style (Figs. 17 and 18). In addition, raised sea shells, water plants and other marine life abound on the various pieces of this magnificent dinner service.

Starting in 1735, and particulary around 1740, Kändler and his associates made a great variety of table decorations, figures and groups of distinct beauty. They include those of the Italian Comedy (Fig. 21), famous court and love scenes with graceful women in "crinoline" alone (Colored Plate IV, page 83, and Fig. 26) or attended by gallant men (Figs. 22, 23, 24 and 25), religious groups (Fig. 27), pastoral youth and adults (Fig. 28) and animal groups (Fig. 29). Various popular characters, birds and animals (Figs. 19 and 20), allegorical groups depicting the arts, crafts and seasons and foreign characters including Turks, Poles, Chinese and Moors were also produced in variable compositions and colors. In addition, MEISSEN produced charming fancy gifts and miniature pieces including snuffboxes, watch cases, cane handles, scent bottles, jewelry cases, buttons, earrings and various other unusual and interesting items.

The artistic decoration reached its highest splendor on the crinoline figures of Kändler (Figs. 22 to 26). These groups were originally designed for banquet table decorations. Under the influence of Höroldt, the earlier ones were painted in brilliant colors while the later ones gave way to lighter hues.

The Baroque fashion evolved into the Regence style about 1725 and then to the Rococo between 1740 and 1750 (Page 21). During this time and later, the heavy vigorous forms and sharp and brilliant Baroque colors (Figs. 16, 18, 30 and 31)

47

were largely replaced by lighter more graceful Rococo forms with harmonious and delicate colors and design (Figs. 33, 34, 35, 36, 37, 40 and 41). MEISSEN began to produce increasing quantities of porcelain decorated with figures, animals, flowers, landscapes and scenes suggested by the paintings of various artists, especially the Frenchman Jean Antoine Watteau (1684-1721) who inspired many pastoral porcelain decorations (Fig. 42), and David Teniers who painted outstanding peasant scenes (Fig. 40).

The factory was placed on a commercial basis about 1750 and produced services and many other items for general domestic use and for export to France, Russia, England, Turkey and other countries. The quality of craftsmanship began to decline as commercial production was emphasized, and many of the pieces lacked artistic appeal. Deterioration continued during the Seven Years War (1756-1763) when a late Rococo fashion prevailed. The victorious Frederick the Great of Prussia made many demands upon Kändler and his associates for services, snuffboxes and special orders, and induced some of the skilled employees including modeler Friedrich Elias Meyer to move to his BERLIN factory.

After peace was declared in 1763, August III and Brühl who had been living in Warsaw, and Höroldt who had fled to Frankfurt, returned to MEISSEN; but the factory was unable to regain its former leadership and production standards. SEVRES captured the primacy of porcelain from MEISSEN while the latter was under the control of Frederick the Great and continued to dominate the field during the last half of the century. BERLIN had improved its position, and six large factories and more than a dozen small ones in Germany and Austria were competing with MEISSEN. The moving spirits, Kändler and Höroldt, had grown old having less imagination and initiative. Höroldt retired in 1765, and both he and his old associate Kändler died at Meissen in 1775.

The "Academic Period," known as the "Point Period" because a point was added to the factory mark, extended from 1763 to 1774 (Mark 6, page 106). According to Honey, "An 'Academic Period' followed the appointment in 1764, as adviser to the factory of the Court-Painter C. W. E. Dietrich, with a constant striving after the Neo-Classical elegance and sentiment. Dietrich naturally favored a pictorial style with the 'Truth to Nature' as its aim. Missions to Sèvres and to other German factories were undertaken in search of models and subjects; in

48

1764, too, a French Sculptor, M. V. Acier, was installed by Kaendler's side as independent *Modellmeister*, and the design department was in charge of J. E. Schönau, who had studied in Paris." Acier produced a number of interesting biscuit and glazed figures (Fig. 39), and much of the other production of this period is charmingly done (Figs. 44 and 45). Kändler continued modeling figures (Fig. 38) and other items until his death, but his work did not measure up to his earlier creations. The Eastern influence had already disappeared, and during this period the European style, especially that of SEVRES, dominated MEISSEN.

Count Camillo Marcolini was designated as MEISSEN's director in 1774 and remained in this position for 40 years. The long period under his direction is referred to as the "Marcolini Period," during which time a star was added below the factory's crossed swords mark (Mark 7, page 106). In spite of the Count's good intentions, he was unable to overcome the accumulated business and technical difficulties of his predecessors. Although attractive pieces of biscuit and porcelain were produced, many of which were in *Louis Seize* or Neo-Classical style, the type and quality were variable and the factory suffered further declines in artistic creation and leadership. The most important painter of the Marcolini period was Johann Georg Loehnig who was called the "first German *Louis Seize* painter" (Fig. 43). The fashions of SEVRES, including its tendency toward Classicism, continued to influence the modeling and painting which had practically reached a period of stagnation. The MEISSEN artists floundered in all directions and with all styles but were unable to create anything truly original. The "Marcolini-Period" ended without distinction with the cessation of the Napoleonic Wars in 1814.

The "1814-1833 Period" following the Napoleonic Wars was associated with a decline in production and little or no improvement in the art. The chrome underglaze-green was developed in 1817 and WEDGWOOD patterns were also produced by the factory. Many of the products were executed in the Empire style of French influence with the excessive use of gold and color. Around 1820 the Biedermeier, *bourgeois*, fashion became prevalent and continued in vogue for about 25 years. During this time, the design and decorations were simpler and characteristic of the middle-class people who had gained prominent recognition at that time.

MEISSEN refers to the period from 1833 to 1870 as the "Kühn Period," after Heinrich Gottlob Kühn who was first chairman and later director of the factory.

The technical and economic position of the enterprise was improved somewhat, and there was a general revival of the great models popular a hundred years earlier. Many figures were copied in Rococo style from the originals to the consternation of collectors. The factory continued to make a large variety of items but few contributions in artistic originality were added.

Beginning about 1870, the so-called "New Period," *die Neuzeit*, began. Penkala writes that, "From 1860 to 1890 the modelers Leuteritz, Hähnel, Ringler, Hirt and Schott were working at MEISSEN. Hirt was the creator of the rather naive and conventional groups of children. Schott modeled figures in Pseudo-Classical style. At the end of the 19th century the sculptor Andresen initiated the so-called 'Youth Style,' *Jugendstil*." A great variety of attractive figures, services and other items, which were copied primarily from earlier models (Figs. 46 and 47), were produced from 1860 on into the 20th century, but they could not claim the splendor of early Baroque and Rococo productions.

After Max Adolf Pfeiffer became director in 1919, Paul Scheurich revived Rococo figures while Paul Börner and Max Esser modeled ultra-modern ones. They along with August Gaul, Ludwig Nick, K. Hentschel, W. Zügel, Willi Münch-Khe and Otto Pilz were responsible for original modeling which stimulated the production of numerous items of real interest (Figs. 48, 49, and 50).

MEISSEN has had its glorious days and periods of depression and decline. It has weathered wars, panics, loss of royal support and numerous other interferences, and rightly deserves international fame for outstanding production over its long and interesting history. Although MEISSEN suffered little material damage as a direct result of World War II, the administration and production were disrupted.

In order to protect its wares against the forgeries of independent decorators, *Hausmaler*, the MEISSEN factory establihed a method of marking its products with the crossed swords, *Kurschwerter*, and other marks soon after 1720. The artists of the factory rarely ever identified themselves by placing their initials or other marks on the pieces which they decorated. The various MEISSEN marks of the different periods are shown on page 106 while similar marks of other factories are illustrated on page 116. An explanation of the prevailing confusion between MEISSEN and "Dresden" porcelain, and the system used in identifying different grades of porcelain are presented on page 103.

VIENNA
(1718 to 1864)

Du Paquier Period (1718-1744): In 1718, the second European porcelain factory was founded in Vienna by the Dutchman Claudius I. Du Paquier through a concession granted by Emperor Charles IV. He was encouraged and assisted by two Meissen deserters—Samuel Stöltzel who knew the production secret, and Konrad Christoph Hunger, an enameler and gilder. Höroldt, the renowned miniature painter, was also employed by Vienna before going to Meissen in 1720.

At first, the paste of Vienna lacked brilliance and whiteness; however, with an improved supply of basic materials the mass was brought to acceptable technical standards. The factory was soon producing porcelain of good glaze and admirable quality although the paste was of a slightly yellow-green tint when compared with that of Meissen.

Hayward reports, "The birth of Vienna porcelain in the year 1718 took place, therefore, at a time when standards of all fields of architecture and representational and applied art were high . . . Du Paquier porcelain has indeed a precious quality." Although information is limited on the able modelers and decorators of the Du Paquier period, some of the most outstanding porcelain specimens were fashioned in Baroque style. J. Folnesics and E. W. Braun are inclined to believe that Ignaz Bottengruber, the famous private porcelain decorator, and some of his followers worked for Vienna between 1730 and 1736 (Page 55). Joseph Philipp Danhofer and Jakob Helkis of Triest also worked as painters during that time.

Hannover classifies the decorations of the "Du Paquier Period" into four divisions, namely: (1) polychromed *chinoiseries* according to the fashion of Höroldt and buds and flowers similar to Japanese Imari, about 1725; (2) polychrome leafy scrolls, *Laub- und Bandelwerk*, with fruits, flowers, canopies, landscapes and figures in panels and *cartouches*, about 1730 to 1740; (3) similar decorations in black, *Schwarzlot*, and gold, from about 1725 to 1740 (Figs. 51 and 52); and (4) pieces decorated in natural German flowers like those of Meissen. Some of the early decorations were of formal oriental flowers and scenes (Figs. 53 and 54). A variety of useful items and some dinner services and independent figures were

51

produced during Du Paquier's time, and small figures were often used as handles of tureen covers (Fig. 51). Although many of the early VIENNA pieces were of Baroque style, the Regence fashion became prominent in the second quarter of the 18th century. The MEISSEN influence on VIENNA is apparent.

STATE PERIOD (1744-1864): Du Paquier sold the factory to the Austrian State in 1744, and it came under the immediate influence of Empress Maria Theresa. It operated thereafter as a Royal-State enterprise, and this period of its production is referred to as the "State Period" (1744-1864). Matthäus Mayerhofer who was director from 1744 to 1764 adopted the Austrian coat of arms as the factory mark, developed a whiter paste of higher grade, employed several outstanding painters and modelers and generally improved the quality of production and financial condition of the establishment. During this period VIENNA employed several able decorators including Christian Daniel Busch, Johann Gottfried Klinger, Philipp Ernst Schindler, all of MEISSEN, and Johann Sigismund Fischer. Technical and artistic trends of MEISSEN were followed and VIENNA gradually became a serious rival to the older institution. The factory profited greatly from the misfortunes of MEISSEN during the Seven Years War, surged to the front and practically conquered the primacy of hard-paste porcelain from the original Saxon factory which had held undisputed leadership for more than a quarter of a century.

Honey reports, "To the first five years (1744-49) belong some grotesque dwarfs, like the 'Callot figures' of Meissen, and miniature Italian Comedy figures of unknown authorship, as well as versions of Kaendler models. Towards 1750 Leopold Dannhauser modelled some 'crinoline groups' and other figures, in a style distinct from that of Meissen; they are often without bases and unpainted. Following these in date and made during a period of more than thirty years came the best-known of all Vienna figures, attributed to Johann Josef Niedermeyer, chief modeller from 1747 to 1784, but possibly due in part to Dannhauser. All have a certain character in common in features and expression and are vivacious dolls with small heads and airy movement." The charming assemblage of figures included doll-like characters (Figs. 55 and 56), mythological subjects of which some were unpainted (Fig. 57), shepherd groups (Fig. 58), lovers (Fig. 59), peddlers, servants, and a large variety of Biblical and allegorical characters. They were principally of Rococo style decorated in light browns, violet, yellow, ivory and various pastel colors. Figure bases were first of different shapes and heights, but around 1765 to 1770 many were mound-like with gold scroll-work decorations (Figs. 58 and 59).

The Rococo style reached its climax and the influence of SEVRES became noticeable by 1765, and increased in emphasis thereafter. Beginning in 1778, Anton Grassi attempted to carry on the superb modeling of Niedermeyer and his associates but his productions were stolid and classical by comparison.

After overcoming financial difficulties, the factory reached its peak of fame under the management of Konrad Sorgenthal between 1784 and 1805. Richly decorated dinner and tea services, vases, plates and similar items were made in the Neo-Classical (Figs. 60 and 62) and Empire (Figs. 61 and 65) styles, inspired by Greek, Roman and Egyptian models. Fine relief decorations in different shades of gold were introduced (Figs. 60 and 61) and beautiful miniature paintings of world famous pictures employed. Cylinder-shaped cups were frequently used for various types of decorations (Figs. 61, 62, 63 and 64). Joseph Leithner who introduced dark colors, and Georg Perl who specialized in gold ornamentation were noted decorators during this period.

The factory started declining after Sorgenthal's death in 1805 with noticeable deterioration in the quality of design and decoration. After a long struggle the famous old institution closed in 1864 after operating for 146 years.

During the "Du Paquier Period" few pieces of original VIENNA porcelain were marked. From 1744 onward, an impressed or an underglaze blue mark which resembles a beehive but which is actually a part of the Austrian coat of arms, the *Bindenschild*, was employed as shown by marks 3 through 5, page 114. From 1783 to 1800 many pieces were dated with two impressed numerals — 83 meaning 1783, 96 specifying 1796 and so on. After 1800 there were three numerals, for example, 803 meaning 1803, and 811 indicating 1811. The VIENNA factory mark has been closely imitated by modern establishments as can be seen on pages 113 and 116.

Marks of other old Austrian porcelain factories including SCHLAGGENWALD, KLOSTERLE, PRAGUE, DALLWITZ, PIRKENHAMMER and ELBOGEN also appear on page 114. These and several other former Austrian factories were embraced in the Checkoslovakian State in 1918. Marks of some later Austrian factories including AUGARTEN which simulated VIENNA forms and marks, appear on page 115.

INDEPENDENT DECORATORS
(Principally from 1715 to 1755)

Soon after the establishment of the MEISSEN and VIENNA factories, there appeared on the market pieces of porcelain which were painted by independent decorators in their homes or studios. Such pieces painted outside of the factory are known as *Hausmalerei,* and the independent painters are called *Hausmaler.* Since the *Hausmalerei* industry developed soon after MEISSEN and VIENNA started operating, it is discussed here in the chronological order of its origin.

Soon after 1720, MEISSEN became concerned about its white porcelain appearing with unfired decorations of outside painters, thereby placing original factory-painted wares in bad repute. It is interesting to note, however, that Böttger and Höroldt are reported to have used the *Hausmaler* of Augsburg as "Guinea pigs." These two MEISSEN directors sent the *Hausmaler* white pieces to be painted in order to gain ideas for painting techniques and decorations.

The *Hausmaler* were experienced painters of faience and other ceramics and the porcelain factories feared their competition. Consequently, MEISSEN started marking its pieces with the letters KPM about 1723 and adopted the blue crossed swords mark around 1724. Despite relentless resistance by the porcelain establishments, the *Hausmaler* were able to obtain MEISSEN, VIENNA and Chinese white porcelain to decorate and dispose of as they saw fit. Intrigue prevailed in the factories to such an extent that whole sets with only one or two bad pieces were often declared defective and sold "in the white" to plant artists and others who decorated and sold the items for profit.

There were limited and varied notions of *Hausmalerei* until Gustav E. Pazaurek's authoritative book of 1925 gave new light on this interesting subject. *Hausmalerei* came into prominence as a result of this revealing publication; however, it should be borne in mind that many of the paintings of independent decorators were also of inferior quality and some are crude forgeries.

Pazaurek reports that the independent decorators of unusual skill were working in at least seven German communities before 1750. In addition, there were dozens of unimportant *Hausmaler* who operated in the same cities and at other places, especially in Dresden where they were very active. Many porcelain decorations,

54

which were believed to have been MEISSEN originals somewhere around the year 1720, particularly the beautiful gold *chinoiseries*, are now known to have been applied several years later by Augsburg goldsmiths who had considerable influence upon MEISSEN decorations. From about 1720 Johann Aufenwerth and his daughter Sabina, who continued working after her father's death in 1728, produced a considerable number of paintings in black monochrome as well as color combinations of red, violet and gold (Fig. 66). Their decorations are sometimes confused with those of Bartholomäus Seuter of Augsburg and his associates who produced many gold Chinese silhouettes. A considerable number of Watteau and rural pictorials, contemporary characters in black or red colors, and multi-colored *chinoiseries* of MEISSEN style were also turned out in Seuter's studio. His portraits were usually framed in scrollwork, laces and dot designs.

Ignaz Bottengruber, a Baroque artist, was the best known of the independent decorators. He and his disciples Hans Gottlieb von Bressler and Karl Ferdinand von Wolfsburg were active in Breslau beginning sometime after 1720 to around 1736 according to their signed and dated pieces. Bottengruber also lived for some years in Vienna beginning about 1730, where he decorated porcelain for the VIENNA factory, and exerted considerable influence upon the art of that establishment during the Du Paquier period. He and his followers specialized in cupids, mythological subjects (Fig. 68), coats of arms, tropics, and combat and sporting scenes. Bottengruber frequently depicted his subjects in single colors of black, red or purple and framed them in characteristic lavish Baroque patterns of gold or polychrome.

Daniel Preissler of Friedrichswalde, Silesia, and his son Ignaz of Kronstadt, Bohemia, conducted a workshop during the second quarter of the 18th century which turned out excellent decorations with almost as much artistic influence as those of Bottengruber. They decorated Chinese and VIENNA porcelain primarily with characteristic *chinoiseries*, and single-tone or black pastorals, hunting groups, festivities and street scenes (Fig. 67).

In Bayreuth, a number of *Hausmaler* including Rudolf Christoph von Drechsel, Johann Friedrich Metzsch, Johann Christoph Jucht, and Joseph Philipp Danhofer from Vienna, decorated porcelain from about 1740 to 1750 in the general style of contemporary MEISSEN. Their decorations varied in color and subject matter.

Landscapes, mythological characters, scenes of harbors, pastorals, flowers and *chinoiseries* were popular among these artists, of whom Metzsch was the most outstanding. Baroque-style frames of various pattern combinations were used to embrace the subjects. As a whole, the decorations of the Bayreuth *Hausmaler* were interesting and of fine quality.

A considerable number of independent decorators operated from about 1740 to 1760 in Saxony and nearby Pressnitz in Bohemia. Generally, their decorations did not compare favorably with those of the Augsburg and Bayreuth *Hausmaler*, and some are considered much inferior. From 1747 to 1766 or later, Franz Ferdinand Mayer painted numerous subjects in his studio including flowers, horsemen, court scenes and dancers (Fig. 70). The decorations were usually of drab colors and generally draped in Baroque frames as were the paintings of many *Hausmaler*.

F. J. Ferner, who is believed to have operated a workshop in Thuringia from about 1745 to 1765, is credited with depicting comparatively crude flowers, buildings and characters on MEISSEN and Thuringian manufactured porcelains. His subjects were framed in plain round or elliptical bands.

The *Hausmaler* were active for a period of approximately 40 years, and some of them carried on their clandestine trade practically under the shadows of the MEISSEN and VIENNA factories. On the other hand, some leading MEISSEN artists painted limited quantities of porcelain privately, despite rigid factory regulations against it. The well-known roving *arcanist* Konrad Christoph Hunger, for example, worked as a *Hausmaler* intermittently in the cities of Meissen and Vienna when not employed in one of the factories. The MEISSEN painter Christian Friedrich Herold was another; and Johann Martin Heinrici who painted at MEISSEN after 1741, and Jakob Helkis (Helchis) who worked for VIENNA around 1740, also painted porcelain outside of their own factories.

The *Hausmalerei* trade was not confined to Germany and Bohemia. Independent decorators operated in Holland and perhaps other countries decorating German, Chinese and any other porcelain they could obtain.

Around 1750 to 1775, a canon of Hildesheim, August Otto Ernst von dem Busch, working just for pleasure as an amateur, decorated white MEISSEN porcelain with scenes of ruins, landscapes, flowers, birds and other subjects. His work was most individualistic (Fig. 69) in that he engraved his subjects upon glazed porcelain with a diamond point stylus and applied black paint in the crevices. His designs appeared as etchings and are extremely dainty and interesting. Many of his productions were signed and dated, and are eagerly sought after by collectors who are willing to pay exorbitant prices.

The best period of the independent painters was from the beginning of MEISSEN to about 1755, by which time the *Hausmalerei* production became so common that it practically ceased to be profitable. The several porcelain factories were doing excellent art work, presenting serious competition to the independent decorators. Later on it became increasingly difficult for the *Hausmaler* to acquire first grade porcelain, as the principal factories had adopted the practice of identifying their discarded white pieces by engraving one or more slashes across their trade marks. Although the *Hausmaler* covered the slashes with gilding or applied their names or initials over the disfigured marks, they were unable to erase evidence that the white pieces had been discarded from factories because of inferior quality.

The relative importance and influence of *Hausmaler* on the overall production of artistic porcelain cannot be accurately ascertained. No doubt, they influenced the techniques, nature and quality of factory decorations to a considerable extent. Pazaurek appropriately compares the influence of the *Hausmaler* to " a pike in the fish pond" in that their competition kept the factory painters on the alert, forcing them to strive for excellence.

The present vogue of collecting *Hausmalerei* is due primarily to the interest created by Pazaurek's book. However much the independent decorators may have confounded the factories and confused the collectors, such artists as Bottengruber, Preissler, Aufenwerth, von dem Busch and many of their associates, have created artistic pieces which have provided an interesting field for collectors.

The production of the *Hausmalerei* appears to have been an artistic expression and a logical outlet of their interests in an art which had attracted widespread attention. In their own individual ways, they made interesting if not always artistic contributions to the porcelain industry.

In addition to the factory mark, if one is present, many pieces of *Hausmalerei* bear dates, symbols and the decorator's initials or full names which may be helpful in identification. The style of design and color arrangement are also factors in determining authorship.

HÖCHST

(1746 to 1796)

With the consent of Elector Friedrich Karl of Mainz, the third great German porcelain establishment was founded by Frankfurt capitalists at near-by Höchst in 1746 in connection with a faience factory. Adam Friedrich von Löwenfink, a former MEISSEN painter, was associated with the new establishment until 1749. The production of hard-paste porcelain began about 1750 under the leadership of Johann Benckgraff from VIENNA, with the assistance of Joseph Jakob Ringler, formerly of MEISSEN (Page 17). The early efforts of the factory were far from successful. Benckgraff left in 1753 for FÜRSTENBERG, the Höchst factory was bankrupt by 1756, and it was not until 1765, when Elector Emmerich Joseph von Breidbach (1763-74) became principal stock holder, that the establishment was properly financed and organized.

The first porcelain paste of HÖCHST was greyish in tone and inconsistent in quality. It was eventually developed into a high-quality creamy-white mixture. The glaze was also transformed into a clear brilliant material in a few years, proving an excellent base for on-the-glaze decorations.

Definite information is not available on the early artists of the factory. Johann Simon Feylner is credited with making simple square-pedestal allegorical groups between 1749 and 1753. During this time Johann Zeschinger, the son-in-law of Benckgraff was also engaged. Johann Friedrich Lück who worked at HÖCHST before 1758, is believed to have made interesting figures and groups including some with Rococo-scrolled bases and trellis-arbours (Fig. 71). A different and typical HÖCHST type of figure was produced sometime between 1758 and 1767 when Lorenz Russinger was chief modeler. Included were Chinese groups (Figs. 72 and 73) and children and pastoral figures which began to show the *Louis Seize* style.

The figures produced by the aforementioned artists received popular acclaim throughout Europe, but it was not until Johann Peter Melchior (1742-1825), a truly great young sculptor, came to HÖCHST that the factory reached its greatest fame. Melchior, a close friend of Goethe (1749-1832), served as *Modellmeister* between 1767 and 1779. In paying tribute to the artistic ability of Melchior, G. B. McClellan, an outstanding American collector of German porcelain, wrote,

"Melchior was the third in ability and chronologically the last of the famous trinity of porcelain modelers which includes, besides himself, Kändler and Bustelli . . While lacking the charm of Bustelli and the marvelous variety of Kändler, his work has an individuality quite its own and is forceful, graceful and distinguished. Without him Höchst would have been little more than a follower of Meissen. Thanks to his achievements it stands out as one of the great factories."

Melchior's figures were warm, animated and often sentimental. They were produced in great variety including sacred or religious groups (Fig. 74), children (Figs. 75, 76 and 77), pastoral and harvest scenes (Fig. 78) and mythological characters (Fig. 79). Melchior and his associates and successors often fashioned the pedestals of their figures as green moss-covered mounds. At first the pieces were painted in light bright colors, with pale harmonious blues predominating, which were frequently applied as designs with spots and stripes. A progressively darker palette was employed in subsequent years. Light rose and pinks were the most prominent and pleasing colors used by Melchior on his delightful figures of children. During his later years, the old master devoted considerable attention to the production of unpainted biscuit figures.

The early modeling and decorations of Höchst porcelain revealed many noticeable characteristics of Meissen wares. Landscapes, Chinese and indigenous scenes and characters, and birds and flowers were the principal subjects portrayed. Scattered flowers and combinations, wreaths and festoons, and mosaic patterns often played a major or supporting role. Pastel and darker polychromes and frequently single colors of crimson, red or black depicted the subjects which were framed in fancy borders of multicolors or gold (Fig. 80). Lavishly fashioned vases in Rococo style (Fig. 81), and simpler and yet pleasing services, cups and saucers (Fig. 82) and odd pieces (Figs. 83 and 84) were painted in cheerful colors. The later designs of Höchst were influenced by the Neo-Classical trend.

By the time Elector Friedrich Karl von Erthal took the factory over in 1778, it had reached the peak of its artistic production, and declined when Melchior departed for Frankenthal in 1779. Many difficulties, especially those of a financial and political nature, confronted the establishment. It was closed in 1796, sold in 1798, and its molds were acquired in 1840 by the pottery of Daniel Ernst Müller at Damm near Aschaffenburg. The Damm factory operated for a number of years and produced faience primarily. Damm pieces made from the former HÖCHST molds are very similar to HÖCHST porcelain, bear the same wheel factory mark with the letter D, and in many instances are falsely represented as such.

During the first years of operation the HÖCHST factory mark, a small electorial wheel with 5 or 6 spokes, usually appeared on the glaze in red, gold, blue or black; but in some instances the wheel mark was impressed without color in the material before firing and glazing. Beginning about 1762 and 1765, respectively, a larger wheel without or with the electorial crown and in various sizes appeared in blue under the glace. HÖCHST porcelain has been imitated on a large scale as several modern factories have copied its styles and used a similar factory mark. The marks of original HÖCHST porcelain appear from 17 to 20, page 106. Similar marks of other factories are shown as marks 4 and 6 on pages 110 and 112, respectively, and all are compared on page 116.

NYMPHENBURG
(1747 to Present Date)

The Bavarian Elector Maximilian III Joseph, whose wife was the granddaughter of August the Strong, provided in 1747 a site for a porcelain factory in a small hunting castle at Neudeck ob der Au, a suburb of Munich. General production began in 1753 when the factory was taken over by the Elector. He appointed Sigismund von Haimhausen (Fig. 91) director. Joseph Jakob Ringler, formerly of the VIENNA factory, served as *arcanist* until he was discharged in 1757, and was succeeded by Johann Paul Rupert Härtl. Incidentally, Ringler who had intended to go to America, became director of the LUDWIGSBURG factory in 1759, (Pages 17, 18 and 74), and remained in that position until 1802.

In 1761, the new factory was transferred from Neudeck to facilities on the Nymphenburg Palace compound, in Munich, where it has operated until the present date. By 1765, NYMPHENBURG had become the outstanding European hardpaste porcelain establishment with approximately 300 employees. However, financial difficulties and the hard times associated with the famine of 1770-71 curtailed its production and reduced the staff of workers to thirty.

Maximilian III Joseph died in 1777 and was succeeded by his distant cousin Karl Theodor (Page 71), Elector of the Palatinate and owner of the successful FRANKENTHAL factory. Karl Theodor favored the FRANKENTHAL factory at the expense of NYMPHENBURG which almost ceased to exist during his tenure. Upon his death in 1799, Maximilian IV Joseph became Elector and was determined to restore porcelain production in NYMPHENBURG to its former importance. The FRANKENTHAL factory ended its operation in 1799 and many of its workmen moved to NYMPHENBURG which entered a period of increased production and prosperity. In 1862 the royal establishment was leased to private operators, and since 1887 it has been under the successful management of the Bäuml family.

According to Honey, "The porcelain of the best period was milk white, fine-grained and practically flawless, though the glaze occasionally shows a greenish tone when pooled in the hollows.

"The fame of Nymphenburg porcelain in modern times has depended almost entirely on the figures modelled for it by Franz Anton Bustelli, a Swiss, between 1754 and 1763 ... His art was remarkable for fantastic invention and a highly personal simplification of form. Figures and draperies are resolved into systems of related planes showing throughout a sensitive play of line; bases are generally flat, airily rising in flowing curves to take a part in the whole delicately balanced composition in a manner never attempted elsewhere."

Practically nothing is known about the life and background of Bustelli (1723-1763), but his genious in the fashioning of figures placed him among the immortals when his work was fully appreciated. Some consider him the greatest figure modeler of all times and that his creations even excelled the figures designed by Kändler, the great *Modellmeister* of MEISSEN, who was sometimes inclined to fashion grotesque monstrosities from porcelain. Bustelli was strictly a modeler of the Rococo style who knew the limitations of porcelain production, and stuck to his specialty of designing graceful life-like figures of all descriptions.

In commenting on the excellent style and performance of Bustelli, Warren E. Cox wrote, "His figures became more and more vital and overflowing with life. Those from the Italian Comedy dance and turn their heads with the most capricious and Latin characteristics and truly they show by contrast how heavy is the Teuton conception of such things; but the genre subjects are as alive and the street vendors, flower girls, fish mongers, cheese sellers and Chinese figures are all personalities into which he breathed life. His children are especially humorous and the putti very naughty and gay. There is in his work an extravagant turn or drop of the head to one side and an accompanying shrug of the shoulder which is over-coy . . . He seems to rise above his day and make fun of the gentlemen and so charming ladies kissing the tips of their fingers, flirting behind fans and reading love letters with a bashful smile."

Bustelli's best known works were the great variety of small figures intended for table decorations. They include characters from the Italian Comedy (Figs. 85, 86, 89 and 90), ladies in crinoline (Fig. 88) and in native costume (Fig. 93), gallant men (Colored Plate II), busts of contemporary personalities (Fig. 91), children, and groups of peasants and Asiatic peoples (Fig. 92). Not all of Bustelli's figures were gay and coquettish, some being Madonnas and characters of a sentimental nature as shown by the Mater Dolorosa (Fig. 87).

Both the modeling and the decorations of Bustelli figures are most pleasing. Some were finished in the white (Figs. 89 and 90), but a majority were decorated with distinct colors (Figs. 85, 86 and 93) including black, red, pink and blue. Sparse paintings were applied on some figures while others were heavily decorated.

The polygonal and Rococo scroll-shaped bases of Bustelli's figures are characteristically thin and flat and rise in flowing curves to support the whole delicately balanced composition in a fashion never achieved by other modelers.

In commenting upon Bustelli, who died in 1763, McClellan wrote, "He appeared without warning from the unknown, wrought wonderously for a decade, and then returned from whence he came, leaving behind him no record of himself except in the creations of his hand and soul."

Dominikus Auliczek became chief modeler in 1764. He was a well-trained sculptor, familiar with the academic essentials, but had limited feeling for the medium of porcelain. He was disposed to copy ideas of others and produced a number of refined and attractive models which were inclined to be of distinct Classical style. Among some of his best works were animal groups (Fig. 95). Auliczek was pensioned in 1797 and succeeded by Johann Peter Melchior who had achieved fame at Höchst between 1767 and 1779 before going to Frankenthal. Melchior served as chief modeler at Nymphenburg between 1797 and 1822,

Plate II Cavalier at Pedestal, by F. A. Bustelli. About 1755 (Page 62).
Bayerisches Nationalmuseum, Munich

NYMPHENBURG

during which time he produced a number of interesting pieces many of which were biscuit portraits and busts (Figs. 100 and 101). However, he had spent most of his artistic ingenuity of Höchst and Frankenthal and contributed little.

From about 1755 to 1767, the factory produced useful porcelains which were most beautiful and of excellent quality. However, these wares never received adequate attention as they were overshadowed by the figures of Bustelli which were produced during most of the same period. A great variety of tablewares (Figs. 96 and 97), snuffboxes, walking cane handles, vases, and other useful and household items were sensitively decorated in Rococo fashion with formal or natural birds, figures, pastorals, and fruits and flowers in charming colors. A special product of Nymphenburg is the food warmer which is a rare collector's item (Fig. 98). Most of the articles produced at that time are eagerly sought by collectors and are becoming increasingly rare and expensive.

During the last quarter of the 18th century, the modeling and decoration followed the prevailing fashion trends with noticeable deterioration in quality. The styles were considerably influenced by the Neo-Classical trend during the last part of the 18th century (Fig. 94). The Empire and Biedermeyer fashions (Fig. 99) became prominent in the first part of the 19th century.

The Nymphenburg manufactory survived the competition and changes of the 19th century but, like all other factories, declined in artistic production. In spite of difficulties it has contributed its share of fine porcelain to the world markets and has been one of the leading factories in adjusting its styles and production to the trends of the time. In recent years the factory has made pure white figures from its old models and a number of new forms has been produced both in color and in white. Several modern modelers, of whom Joseph Wackerle was one of the most prominent, produced attractive figures and groups which have been favorably received (Fig. 102). The modern production of the factory is of great variety and of good quality when compared with international standards.

The marks of Nymphenburg are comparatively reliable in determining the age of porcelain items, since most of the production periods are indicated by the size or shape of the Bavarian shield and the direction of the lozenges or cross hatches on it. The shield marks are impressed without color and are usually exposed on the pedestals of the figures. The various shield marks, the blue underglaze hexagram mark, and the modern marks of NYMPHENBURG are shown at the top of page 107. NYMPHENBURG also produces figures from FRANKENTHAL models which are marked as explained on page 72.

FÜRSTENBERG
(1747 to 1859, Royal-State · 1859 to Date, Private)

The FÜRSTENBERG factory was founded in the castle of Fürstenberg in 1747 by Karl I, Duke of Brunswick. There was really no reason for establishing this factory in the absence of raw materials, trained craftsmen and demand, except to satisfy the vanity of the persistent Duke. Porcelain was not produced, however, until 1753 at which time several HÖCHST artists were procured. They included Johann Benckgraff as *arcanist* and director, Simon Feylner as modeler and color chemist and Johann Zeschinger as decorator. Production and financial problems, accompanied with the death of Benckgraff soon after his arrival, prevented the factory from operating normally until about 1770.

The paste and glaze materials which came from the great distance of Passau were at first greyish in tone and often faulty because of impurities. Consequently, many of the pieces were overdecorated in order to cover the defects. After about 1770 the grey color was eliminated and the paste approximated the whiteness, density and texture of MEISSEN porcelain. Likewise the original spotty greyish-glaze was brought to a clear brilliant consistency after some experience, and a satisfactory combination of paste and glaze resulted.

Prominent modelers, in addition to *Modellmeister* Feylner who served from 1753 to 1770, were Johann Christoph Rombrich (1758-94), Anton Karl Luplau (1765-76), the Frenchman Desoches (1769-74), Karl Gottlieb Schubert (1778-1804) and P. Hendler. Feylner modeled some very good Italian Comedy characters, miners and Greek Gods, but until almost 1770 the production of figures was limited, primarily because of difficulties in handling the paste. In the 1760's Rombrich and Desoches modeled biscuit portrait plaques and busts from life as well as some from Greek poets, philosophers and statesmen oftentimes in the WEDGWOOD manner Luplau did Greek figures and conventional groups (Fig. 103). Schubert was responsible for some interesting equestrian statuettes, and a variety of other subjects were produced by the several modelers. The chief decorators of the 18th century included Andreas Oest, Johann Heinrich Eisenträger, C. G. Albert, Christ Luplau, Johann Friedrich Weitsch, and Heinrich Christian Brüning who with the staff of modelers did some outstanding work which spread the fame of the factory.

According to Christian Scherer and other writers, the artists of FÜRSTENBERG are reputed to have imitated many models and decorations of other factories. It is one of the few establishments which adopted styles from such English factories as BOW, CHELSEA, and WEDGWOOD. The influence of SEVRES, MEISSEN and BERLIN is noticeable in many of their productions. However, in high-relief and round modeling the artists showed considerable originality in their figures, services, vases and other ornamental objects.

FÜRSTENBERG was never outstanding in figure production; however, its vases (Figs. 105 and 107) after 1760 are famous, and the services and various useful and decorative items compete with those of other 18th century factories. In the early years of operation, exquisite Rococo paintings resembling those o MEISSEN and BERLIN were applied on tablewares in relief and in beautifully decorated *rocaille* frames on flat surfaces (Fig. 104). Charming landscapes and Watteau scenes (Fig. 105), and life-like paintings of fowls (Fig. 106) were prominent.

Although FÜRSTENBERG, like other factories, suffered as a result of the Seven Years War, the best period of the establishment extended from about 1770 to 1790, during which time paste and decorating materials were improved considerably. Beginning about 1768, the palette of enamel colors was extended to include dark green, purple, soft brown and a clear yellow. Gilding was freely employed in the border patterns which were characteristic of the factory.

The predominant influence of Neo-Classicism appeared in the styles of modeling and painting soon after 1775, as is clearly shown by many of the pieces (Fig. 107). The Frenchman Louis Victor Gerverot, who served as director from 1795 to 1814, was also responsible for perpetuating the foreign tastes.

FÜRSTENBERG was leased by the government in 1859, passed into private ownership in 1876, and has continued to operate as a commercial enterprise to the present time. The factory has kept abreast of the times, maintaining a favorable reputation for its great variety of vases, tablewares and other items.

The factory mark, a capital F in script, is painted in blue under the glaze on most items. The medallions have a gold F on the back while the biscuit pieces are impressed with the running horse of Brunswick. The old marks are shown as number 5, 6 and 7 on page 107, and the modern ones are shown in frame 8.

BERLIN FACTORIES
(1751 to 1757 · 1761 to Date)

WEGELY'S FACTORY (1751 to 1757): The first porcelain factory in Berlin was started by Wilhelm K. Wegely in 1751, with the moral and financial support of the Prussian King, Frederick the Great (1712-1786), and the technical aid of *arcanists* and craftsmen from HÖCHST. Ernst Heinrich Reichard served as head modeler and Isaac-Jacques Clauce of MEISSEN as the principal decorator.

The porcelain of the factory was very hard, clean and white, being similar to that of MEISSEN. WEGELY produced services, vases and figures of ordinary characters, which were generally modeled and decorated in the prevailing Rococo style with characteristics of MEISSEN and HÖCHST. Decorating was difficult because the porcelain was so hard, therefore many items were unpainted (Fig. 108). Watteau scenes, landscapes and German flowers in dark red or purple were usually employed on the pieces which were decorated.

In spite of an auspicious beginning, Wegely was unable to satisfy the critical taste of his royal patron who had always viewed the fame of MEISSEN with jealousy. With the loss of Frederick's support and the development of financial difficulties, the discouraged Wegely closed the establishment in 1757.

GOTZKOWSKY'S FACTORY (1761 to 1763): Johann Ernst Gotzkowsky purchased the *arcanum* of porcelain production from Reichard of WEGELY and started a new factory in 1761. With the continuing services of Reichard and Clauce, and the employment of several MEISSEN artists including Friedrich Elias Meyer as chief modeler, and the decorators Carl Wilhelm Böhme, Johann Balthasar Borrmann and Karl Jakob Christian Klipfel, the GOTZKOWSKY factory produced a number of services, tea sets and other items somewhat similar to MEISSEN. The paste was yellowish-grey but of fairly good quality. A considerable number of items were modeled and decorated in MEISSEN manner. Few pieces of this factory exist.

The chief ambition of Frederick the Great was to make BERLIN porcelain equal to or excel that of MEISSEN, so when Gotzkowsky ran into financial difficulties, Frederick bought the factory in 1763 and continued it as a royal enterprise.

KING'S PORCELAIN MANUFACTORY (KPM) (1763 to date): Although Johann Georg Grieninger was appointed director of the royal BERLIN factory in 1763 and continued as such until his death in 1798, it was King Frederick himself who actually conducted the manufactory as he saw fit. Robert Schmidt states, "When Frederick the Great acquired the BERLIN factory from Gotzkowsky, he remained in constant touch with the enterprise, supervised the work critically and ordered a large number of items, especially large table services for the various castles." In any event, the King ran the BERLIN enterprise according to his own ideas and is largely responsible for its successes and deficiencies.

The first porcelain of the BERLIN (KPM) factory was yellowish-grey, but from about 1770 the paste was a clear white mass which produced hard porcelain of good quality. Likewise the glaze was hard, clear, and technically superior which, when added to the white paste made the final product almost a bluish-white.

Frederick the Great retained Reichard, Clauce, Meyer, Borrmann and others who were employed by the WEGELY or GOTZKOWSKY factories, and added serveral other artists who gave him one of the finest technical staffs in Germany. He was determined to make his factory a business as well as an artistic success. For example, the Berlin lotteries were compelled to distribute large quantities of the factory's products, no Jew could obtain a marriage certificate until he had bought a set of BERLIN porcelain, and sales were pushed in many other assiduous ways.

Friedrich Elias Meyer, who was employed between 1761 and 1785, and his brother Wilhelm Christian Meyer between 1766 and 1772, were responsible for most of the figures during their tenure. Their modeling was quite similar, but Wilhelm Christian who was perhaps the abler, was responsible for the more animated figures with dainty heads. The Meyer's and their associates produced various types including mythological groups, figures of native people and sheperds, characters of foreign countries (Fig. 109), cavaliers and pretty ladies (Fig. 110), as well as historical plaques in relief (Fig. 118). Their subjects were usually glazed and decorated, but some were of biscuit (Fig. 111).

The early BERLIN figures were mounted on tripod pedestals, but round, oval and square bases (Figs. 113 and 115) of variable thickness were used by 1775. Although many figures of BERLIN were attractive and of fine quality, they never attained the artistic standards of other leading German factories.

BERLIN's fame is associated with ornamental and useful wares, fruit bowls, clocks (Fig. 112) and other items which were produced in great variety and quantity. The factory is especially noted for its services (Figs. 119, 120 and 121), which were beautifully modeled and decorated. The most famous include those made for the Royal Palace at Potsdam (1765-66) and the Palace at Breslau (1767-68). Exceptionally fine flower paintings, often in Rococo style (Fig. 116), were used in adorning individual pieces. Watteau paintings, battle scenes, historical and group paintings (Figs. 120 and 121) and landscapes were also done with great skill. A variety of interestingly decorated plates of BERLIN and other German manufactories are shown in Figure 117.

Most of the decorations involved various colors and frequently gilding, but some were done in red, purple or other monotones. Well-known oil paintings were reproduced as miniatures on porcelain plaques of various sizes. BERLIN was the first factory to produce lithophanes, which involved designs on biscuit slabs that appear as pictorial subjects under transmitted light.

The Rococo style predominated in the first period of BERLIN (Fig. 116), and beginning about 1770 the factory produced plain vases and other wares with floral decorations in the style of SEVRES. After about 1775 Neo-Classical features prevailed (Fig. 119), evolving into the Empire style in the beginning of the 19th century, during which time gold and color were applied lavishly. The simple Biedermeier influence was evident from about 1820 to 1850 (Fig. 122).

The BERLIN factory was generally successful under the energetic direction of Frederick the Great who had employed an able staff of artists, provided good management, and insisted on good workmanship; but the enterprise started comparatively late to achieve the superlative. By the time Frederick died in 1786, the decadence of artistic porcelain had begun.

The factory continued to produce good quality items, especially dinner services, vases, and other useful and decorative porcelains. Outstanding artists during the first half of the 19th century were Karl Friedrich Schinkel and Hans C. Genelli, for vases and tablewares; Gottlieb Schadow, for figures; Johann Friedrich Riese, for busts of famous living people; and Leonhard Posch, for portrait medallions on cups and vessels. High class production, primarily on a commercial basis, has been carried on to the present date, and BERLIN is considered one of the leading German factories. The modern tablewares of BERLIN are especially attractive and some outstanding figures, mostly in white, were made by Paul Scheurich and his able associates under the direction of Max Adolf Pfeiffer (Fig. 123).

The BERLIN manufactory was practically destroyed during World War II. With improvisations the establishment managed to operate in a limited way, but a large proportion of the production was transferred to Selb, Bavaria.

The mark during Wegely's time was a W in underglaze blue, mark 9, page 107; while Gotzkowsky used a crude G, mark 10, page 107, usually in underglaze blue, but sometimes painted over the glaze in brown, black or gold. The marks of the BERLIN (KPM) porcelain manufactory, beginning in 1763, were underglaze blue in the form of a scepter with variations and additions, according to the period, as shown by marks 11 through 16, page 107. The *Reichsapfel*, a red overglaze stamped mark, was added in 1832 to indicate that the piece had been painted in the factory, mark 16. Since 1913 a green *Reichsapfel* is applied when the piece is decorated in the factory with a gilded rim and simple trimmings.

FRANKENTHAL
(1755 to 1799)

The FRANKENTHAL factory was established in 1755 by Paul Anton Hannong who owned and operated a successful pottery at Strasbourg. Because of the VINCENNES-SEVRES royal monopoly, other French porcelain factories were not permitted to decorate their wares; so with the permission of Elector Karl Theodor of the Palatinate, Hannong selected the German town of Frankenthal, 65 miles north of Strasbourg, as the home of his new factory.

Hannong's sons, Karl and Joseph, managed the new establishment while the father continued at STRASBOURG. Karl died in 1757 and his brother Joseph, who was a modeler, succeeded him as director and purchased FRANKENTHAL from his father in 1759. Because of financial difficulties the factory was sold in 1762 to the Elector. Adam Bergdoll served as director until 1775 and was replaced by Johann Simon Feylner, who had formerly modeled at HÖCHST and FÜRSTENBERG.

The first porcelain of the factory contained Passau clay, was creamy-white and of excellent quality. The thick glaze was technically satisfactory for decorating. From about 1780 the paste was slightly greyish in color.

FRANKENTHAL's early years, from about 1755 to 1775, comprised the best era, during which time a great variety and quantity of items were manufactured. According to Heuser, Hofmann and other writers, more than 800 figures and groups have been identified. Since 600 different items were on exhibition in Munich in 1909, it is believed that a much larger number existed. Carolsfeld reports that figures played the most important production role at FRANKENTHAL as was the case in other South German factories, and with the exception of MEISSEN it produced more figures than any other establishment in the same period.

Some outstanding figures and groups, somewhat similar to the works of MEISSEN but simpler in fashion (Fig. 124), were produced between 1755 and 1761 by Johann Wilhelm Lanz, the first master modeler appointed by Hannong. Some of his figures were based on sparsely decorated mounds while others were supported by beautiful Rococo pedestals (Colored Plate III). Johann Friedrich Lück (1758-64), who presumably succeeded Lanz, is credited with producing somewhat similar figures with characteristic fuller cheeks and a slight air of stiffness (Fig. 125).

When Karl Theodor bought the factory in 1762, he engaged the court sculptor Konrad Link who modeled until 1766 and for short periods thereafter. He produced mythological subjects (Figs. 127 and 128), busts (Fig. 130) and ballet and other figures of distinguished style and quality, both in elaborate colors and plain white (Fig. 131). Karl Gottlieb Lück served as head modeler from 1766 to 1775, during which time he and his associates produced many dainty figures and groups (Figs. 126 and 129), and FRANKENTHAL reached its height of plastic accomplishment. Adam Bauer served as head modeler between 1775 and 1779 and was succeeded by Johann Peter Melchior, of HÖCHST fame, who served until 1793 without making any great contribution to the already excellent collection of models. Melchior was succeeded by Landolin Ohmacht, the last master-modeler of the factory.

For the most part FRANKENTHAL porcelain was excellently decorated in considerable variety. Cloth-pattern designs and gilt-striped decorations were prominent, also combinations of crimson and green colors. Miscellaneous items (Fig. 133) and especially the best vases and tablewares were elaborately painted, often with unusual battle and hunting scenes (Fig. 132), festival subjects (Fig. 134), mythological characters and birds and flowers, often in SEVRES fashion (Fig. 135).

Honey states, "The FRANKENTHAL table-wares and vases of the best period were beautifully finished and were often painted with elaborate figure-subjects of a kind seldom attempted elsewhere in Germany, as well as in versions of the more ordinary MEISSEN styles. Three artists are known by their signed pieces — Winterstein (1758-81) painted subjects after David Teniers amongst others, Jacob Osterspei (1759-82) mythological scenes, while Johann Bernhard Magnus (1762-82) was famous for battle-pieces. The decorative designs are remarkable for chinz-patterns and gilt-striped grounds; trellis and other diapers show a fondness for crimson and green in combination. Cabaret-sets were a favourite form, comprising teapot and tea-cups, cream-jug and sugar-basin, on a lozenge-shaped tray."

The factory came into existence at the best time of the Rococo period, was influenced by the Neo-Classical but closed before the Empire style was in vogue. FRANKENTHAL did its best to rival SEVRES, which strongly influenced its style, especially in the later period of its existence. Although FRANKENTHAL's 44 years of operation was the shortest of any major German factory, its general success is evidenced by its great variety and high quality of products.

FRANKENTHAL was confiscated in 1795 following the French Wars, was leased for a while, and finally closed in 1899. Its leading craftsmen were transferred to NYMPHENBURG (Page 61). Some of the molds were moved to a factory at Grünstadt, while others were acquired later by NYMPHENBURG for reproducing the old forms.

The factory marks for the various periods of FRANKENTHAL appear as numbers 17 through 21 on page 107. The earliest marks were the impressed letter PH for Paul Hannong, a blue lion under the glaze or a lozenge-shield as shown in marks 17, 18 and 19, respectively. When Karl (Charles) Theodor took over the factory in 1762, he employed the combined initials CT under the crown in underglaze blue

Plate III Wine Grower and Companion, by J. W. Lanz, after an Etching by J. E. Nilson.
About 1760 (Page 71). *Bayerisches Nationalmuseum, Munich*

FRANKENTHAL

as indicated by mark number 20. From 1795 the van Recums used their initials as shown in number 21. The NYMPHENBURG factory introduced the blue lion mark and the CT with a crown on their modern FRANKENTHAL modeled pieces. In addition to the old FRANKENTHAL marks, which also bear the year of production, the regular impressed shield mark of the NYMPHENBURG establishment is applied to avoid deception (Page 64).

LUDWIGSBURG
(1758 to 1824)

The LUDWIGSBURG porcelain factory was founded in a town of that name about twelve miles north of Stuttgart in 1758 by Karl Eugen, the free-spending luxury-loving Duke of Württemberg. Joseph Jakob Ringler, the well-known roving *arcanist*, formerly from the VIENNA and NYMPHENBURG manufactories, was appointed director in 1759 and remained in that capacity for more than 40 years. It was under Ringler's able management that the expensive enterprise satisfied the vanity of the Duke and enjoyed varying degrees of artistic success. Like some other factories, however, it had no real excuse for existence except to increase the magnificence of its protector.

It was necessary to transport the ingredients of the paste from the distant vicinity of Passau. The finished porcelain was seldom white, but of a smoky-tone or yellowish-grey tint. Although the paste lacked mechanical perfection it was cohesive and well adapted to modeling. As a rule, overdecoration was required in order to cover up the defects. The glaze was often of a green tint and uneven but was transparent and of good quality.

According to Adolf Brüning, the early designs of the factory were copied primarily from MEISSEN pieces in the collection of Duke Karl Eugen; however, the artists soon developed a pronounced LUDWIGSBURG style of their own. The greal luxury of the Ludwigsburg court and ballet provided sufficient imagination and inspiration for the modelers to produce original and interesting artistic subjects. The Rococo style prevailed in the beginning, being followed in turn by the

Neo-Classical and Empire influence in keeping with changing fashions. Everything considered, the best period of the factory was from about 1760 to about 1775.

Gottlieb Friedrich Riedel, who had previously worked with MEISSEN, HÖCHST and FRANKENTHAL played the major role in all designing and modeling from about 1759 to 1779. He and his associates produced interesting mythological, Classical and other figures (Fig. 136), useful wares often decorated with birds, and ornamental articles such as candlesticks (Fig. 141). His subjects were primarily in Rococo style and were frequently supported with trellis-backgrounds. Riedel also influenced the work of other factories since he left behind many well preserved engravings, sketches and designs. Johann Göz worked from 1759 to 1762 with Riedel as figure modeler. Domenico Ferretti and Pierre-François Lejeune, court sculptors, also prepared models for the factory at times between 1762 and 1767.

Jean-Jacques Louis of Namur, who was a repairer under Riedel's direction until his death in 1772, is believed to have produced some charming spirited dancing figures with Rococo pedestals. According to Honey, Louis is also responsible for "some very delightful miniature groups of peasants and tradesmen with their booths and sideshows; these 'Venetian Fair groups' (which are among the best of all porcelain figures) are said to have been suggested by the fairs instituted by the Duke on his return from Venice in 1767.

"The strongest influence, however, was that of the famous court-sculptor, Johann Christian Wilhelm Beyer, who was definitely appointed to the oversight of the modelling workshop in 1764. But the marks of his style are recognizable in figures that may be earlier than this. Some masterly small figures of folk-types-peasants, howkers, workpeople, etc., of about 1760—65, in posture and turn of body already recall Beyer's preference; they are monumental in spite of their small scale. With their characteristic rhythm and delicate subdued coloring in tones of brownish red, light blue and pale yellow, shared with the ballet groups, these figures rank among the best of their kind." Beyer's creations were usually of Rococo fashion or with Classical tendencies, and of considerable variety. He also modeled fishermen (Fig. 137), soothsayers, singers (Fig. 138), wine drinkers (Fig. 139), musicians (Fig. 140) and other subjects usually with delightfully twisted bodies. He is reported to have made table decorations and other items before going to Vienna in 1767.

Although modeling was highly developed, reflecting the influence of the Court of Württemberg, the figures of LUDWIGSBURG as a whole do not measure up in quality to those produced by MEISSEN, NYMPHENBURG, FRANKENTHAL and perhaps HÖCHST and FULDA. The later LUDWIGSBURG biscuit and glazed figures are of limited interest since many were made from earlier models and placed on square bases while others were fashioned in Neo-Classical style (Fig. 142).

LUDWIGSBURG also produced a variety of tablewares, vases, and other ornamental items in Rococo style during the earlier years of operation. Elaborately decorated tea-pots (Fig. 143), vases, urns (Fig. 144), and three-legged coffee-pots are typical products of the factory. Tablewares decorated with *rocaille* ornaments in relief and white osier (basket weave) patterns (Fig. 145) are characteristic of the charming Rococo period. Classicism influenced the styles and decorations from about 1770 (Fig. 146). Johann Friedrich Schmidt was a prominent designer of vases and useful wares and Friedrich Kirschner specialized in flower painting.

The general quality of LUDWIGSBURG porcelain started declining soon after 1770. The factory was never profitable or highly successful, so when its patron Duke Karl Eugen died in 1793, production deteriorated more rapidly. After struggling along for 30 years the factory closed in 1824. LUDWIGSBURG molds are reported to have been sent first to Regensburg in 1825; and later, about 1850, to an Amberg pottery which made some poor copies.

The factory mark from 1759 to 1793 consists of two C's which were overlapped back-to-back, in blue under the glaze, with or without a crown as shown by marks 1 through 7, page 108. Some of the LUDWIGSBURG pieces were also marked with an odd-shaped S, alone or in addition to the usual mark. Three antlers were employed from 1770 to 1775. From 1793 to about 1800, an old-fashioned L was used frequently without the crown (Mark 8, page 108). The letters FR (Frederick Rex) with or without a crown were employed from about 1806 to 1816 (Mark 9). From 1816 to 1824, the letters WR (Wilhelm Rex) appeared usually in gold under the crown (Mark 10).

The *Württembergische Porzellan-Manufaktur,* at Schorndorf, produced porcelain after old LUDWIGSBURG models for a number of years preceding World War II. The products were labeled with the factory marks of LUDWIGSBURG and the additional letters WPM as shown in frame 18 on page 112.

CHAPTER IV

Other Porcelain Factories

In addition to the eight major German porcelain factories which were discussed in Chapter III, at least twenty minor or small manufactories were established in German provinces during the last half of the 18th century. Best known of them are ANSBACH, KELSTERBACH, OTTWEILER, FULDA, KASSEL, GUTENBRUNN, GOTHA, KLOSTER VEILSDORF, VOLKSTEDT, WALLENDORF, LIMBACH, ILMENAU, GERA, GROSSBREITENBACH, RAUENSTEIN and several others.

Some of these smaller factories were started by princes, but a majority were established as private commercial enterprises for the purpose of producing the kind of wares which could be sold at a profit in competition with other factories. Because of commercial emphasis and the fact that most of the smaller enterprises opened after the general art of porcelain had started declining, no great artistic contribution was made by them. For the most part they followed the production methods and styles of the older major factories; however, some produced original high quality products. Several of these factories existed for only a few years; but a majority of them, particularly those near the sources of raw materials, have continued to operate despite economic disruptions, changes of ownership and competition offered by the large number of commercial enterprises which were established in the 19th and 20th centuries.

As some collectors and dealers are particularly concerned with the products of one or more of these establishments, and most are interested in the history of all of them, they are discussed briefly in the chronological order of their establishment. Their geographical positions are shown on the map, page 41.

ANSBACH

(1758 to 1860)

The ANSBACH porcelain factory was established in connection with an old faience works in Ansbach in 1758 with the aid and patronage of Hohenzollern Margrave Alexander of Brandenburg. *Arcanist* Johann Friedrich Kändler, a cousin of the great MEISSEN Kändler, is believed to have started production with the help of other MEISSEN workers. The enterprise was moved to the princely hunting castle at Bruckberg in 1762, and produced its outstanding pieces during the Rococo period until about 1775. Following the Margrave's abdication in 1791 in favor of his cousin, the factory started declining. ANSBACH was sold to private interests in 1807, but continued operations until it closed in 1860.

The porcelain paste of ANSBACH was very pure and white and the glaze was of comparatively fine quality. This combination made it possible to produce a variety of interesting and attractive items.

Information is limited on the artists. Kändler, the first manager, is believed to be responsible for some of the figures with characteristic straight noses. His successor, the modeler Carl Gottlob Laut, and Johann F. Scherber are credited with exotic groups and figures, comedians, demigods, allegories and lovers with typical angular heads and pointed noses. Many of the figures, especially those with characteristic smiling faces and puffy eyes, are of unusual quality. Both white and painted figures (Figs. 148 and 149) were made in considerable variety.

Of special interest are the decorative and useful wares, particularly the coffee-pots with their delicate figure-faced spouts and beautiful decorations (Fig. 147). Souvenir plates, monogrammed cups and saucers (Fig. 150), and silhouetted medallions of excellent quality were also produced. Outstanding paintings in purple and pale blue, including Watteau scenes in *rocaille* frames of dainty gold lace, were made by chief painter Johann Melchior Schöllhammer. He was assisted by Johann Stenglein who specialized in Dutch landscapes, and Schreitmüller and Kahl who were flower painters.

In some respects the products of ANSBACH are original in character. However, many of its items, especially the useful wares, have features of form and decoration which are similar to BERLIN and NYMPHENBURG and sometimes MEISSEN.

ANSBACH porcelain is displayed in most of the European museums and sought by collectors. The largest collection existing at the time of this writing – about 800 pieces including figures, vases, tea-pots, plates, cups and saucers – is in the possession of Adolf Bayer of Ansbach, near Nürnberg, who is a genial host, enthusiastic collector, and the author of the book "*Ansbacher Porzellan.*"

The factory marks appear as numbers 11 through 15, page 108. All of the marks shown are underglaze blue except number 14 which is impressed without color and is primarily used for making figures. The principal mark from about 1760 to 1785 was an A of varying sizes and shapes, signifying Alexander the Margrave and not Ansbach as is commonly thought. The rare, variable-sized Brandenburg Eagle mark, frame 15 page 108, is believed to have been used primarily on *Geschirre* for the court of the Margrave sometime between 1762 and 1785.

KELSTERBACH
(1761 to 1768 and 1789 to 1802)

KELSTERBACH was started by Christian Daniel Busch from a faience factory on the Main river in 1761 for Ludwig VIII, the Landgrave of Hessen-Darmstadt. Busch continued as *arcanist* and painter until 1765. Karl Vogelmann modeled interesting primitive-type figures somewhat in HÖCHST style sometime before 1765 (Fig. 151). Peter Anton Seefried is reported to have made more than fifty models in white glaze between 1766 and 1768, primarily imitations of Bustelli's NYMPHENBURG figures. Some decorated services-often in plain Classical style-snuffboxes, and other useful and decorative items were also produced.

The paste was usually of a yellowish tint. Good quality porcelain was made until about 1768 when operations ceased. In 1789 *arcanist* Jakob Melchior Höckel assisted in reviving the establishment which finally closed in 1802. Many KELSTER-BACH items resemble those of HÖCHST, FRANKENTHAL and NYMPHENBURG.

The pieces during the time of Busch (1761-65) were unmarked. From 1765 to 1768, the letters HD (Hessen-Darmstadt) with a crown were used, while only the letters HD were used in blue under the glaze in the second period, 1789-1802, as shown in frames 19 and 20 on page 108.

OTTWEILER

(1763 to about 1770-75)

In 1763, the OTTWEILER factory, sometimes referred to as NASSAU-SAARBRÜCKEN, was established for Prince Wilhelm Heinrich of Nassau-Saarbrücken, with the aid of *arcanist* Dominique Pellevé from Rouen. The establishment passed into private hands upon the death of Prince Wilhelm Heinrich in 1769, but carried on the production of porcelain to about 1775. Thereafter, the factory operated as a pottery until it closed in the year 1797.

OTTWEILER porcelain was of variable whiteness and quality with a satisfactory glaze. The near-by French influence was noticeable in the modeling and decorations of its *Geschirre*. Although the factory was not outstanding, some of its table and useful wares were admirably decorated with various character subjects in Rococo gilded frames (Fig. 158) or relief (Fig. 159). Friedrich Karl Wohlfahrt who previously worked for HÖCHST, FRANKENTHAL and GUTENBRUNN, was employed as painter around 1769 to 1771 and is responsible for some very attractive decorations (Fig. 160). Some figures were produced but they are very rare like all pieces of the factory.

The NS mark shown in frame 5 on page 109 stands for NASSAU-SAARBRÜCKEN. Sometimes the letter W appears under the NS mark.

FULDA

(1765 to 1790)

The FULDA manufactory was established in 1765 for Heinrich von Bibra, Prince-Bishop of Fulda, with the assistance of Nikolaus Paul who was formerly employed at the WEGELY factory in Berlin. FULDA's finest products were made before 1780 at which time it may have closed, although some writers report that it continued to operate until 1790.

A fine quality white paste and a sparkling glaze were employed in producing pieces of great charm. The predominant style was of the late Rococo period with a tendency towards *Louis Seize* taste which prevailed at that time.

According to Maria Penkala, "Specimens of the plastic art of this factory are of great artistic value. Graceful figures were produced as well as very natural groups in Rococo style on a rounded base resembling the best FRANKENTHAL products. The painting was particularly artistic and colorful. Figures produced at FULDA are very rare and valuable."

Information on the excellent modeling of FULDA is rather indefinite. Hofmann states that Johann Baptist Xaveri was *Modellmeister* about 1770. Honey and Arno Schönberger are inclined to believe that Lorenz Russinger is also responsible for some of the FULDA figures as they are very similar to those produced by him while modeling at HÖCHST.

FULDA's figures and groups were of outstanding quality and of considerable variety. Principal subjects include sheep herders, children in various poses, charming ladies and cavaliers (Figs. 152 and 155), comedians (Fig. 153), and attractive groups framed on Rococo trellises (Fig. 154). Fashioning was simple and dainty yet unusually distinctive. Although many of the figures resemble those produced by HÖCHST, the later models include versions of the FRANKENTHAL factory.

Services and special items (Figs. 156 and 157) were also of excellent quality and were frequently decorated with single colors of lavender or reddish brown. Considering the total production of the enterprise, many authorities rate the quality of FULDA products with that of the leading major factories. In fact, it is believed by some connoisseurs that the rare figures of FULDA are excelled in beauty and value only by those of MEISSEN and NYMPHENBURG.

Factory marks are usually a double F with or without a crown in underglaze blue (Frames 6 and 8, page 109). A few pieces are marked with a simple cross.

KASSEL
(1766 to 1788)

This small factory which operated between 1766 and 1788 was founded by Friedrich II, Landgrave of Hessen-Kassel, who was assisted by Nikolaus Paul, a former FULDA technician. Nothing unusually original was made by KASSEL which produced attractive tablewares primarily in underglaze blue and of simple taste. J. G. Pahland from FÜRSTENBERG is credited with modeling some figures, most of which are white, but some are decorated (Fig. 161). The pieces of this factory are rare and not often seen in German antique shops. The marks, a lion or HC (Hessen-Cassel) in underglaze blue, are shown in frame 9, page 109.

GUTENBRUNN
(1767 to 1775)

This factory, often referred to as PFALZ-ZWEIBRÜCKEN, was established with the help of Duke Christian IV of Pfalz-Zweibrücken in 1767, and was moved to Gutenbrunn in 1769. Lorenz Russinger came from HÖCHST to start operations. Upon leaving for France in 1768 he was succeeded by Johann Melchior Höckel, an *arcanist* who worked at times for KELSTERBACH. Nothing unusual was initiated by the factory which specialized in simple useful wares made from local kaolin and painted with flowers. However, some of the best pieces made from Passau clay were attractively decorated with flowers, landscapes, and harbor scenes (Fig. 162). The PZ (Pfalz-Zweibrücken) factory mark is shown in frame 10, page 109.

WÜRZBURG
(1775 to 1780?)

A porcelain and faience factory is reported to have been opened in Würzburg in 1775 by Johann Caspar Geyer who received the concession from the Prince-Bishop of Würzburg, Adam Friedrich von Seinsheim. Geyer died five years later, and there is limited evidence as to the quality or scope of production of this short-lived establishment. Honey has written that, "Table-wares were carefully painted with landscapes with figures often having gilt scrollwork below, *Mosaik* in BERLIN style, *Louis Seize* garlands, and Classical figures in *camaieu*." Some pieces, dating somewhere around 1775 to 1780, depicting Würzburg scenes, are reported to exist.

There is also some confusion about the factory marks. The CGW mark for Caspar Geyer, Würzburg and a W symbol are shown in frame 13, page 109.

Plate IV Lady in Crinoline, by J. J. Kändler. About 1740 (Page 47).
Museum für Kunst und Gewerbe, Hamburg

MEISSEN

THE THURINGIAN FACTORIES
(1757 Onward)

Between 1757 and 1783, nine hard-paste porcelain establishments were founded in favorably located forested sections of Thuringia which had a good supply of fuel, water power and raw porcelain materials. These factories have much in common in that most of them were founded on a commercial basis to supply the great demand for useful porcelain. All were established by businessmen except KLOSTER VEILSDORF and, as a whole, they have enjoyed varying degrees of financial success. With the exception of GOTHA each was owned at one time or another by some member of the Greiner family, and all have been reported as operating to the present date with minor interruptions and changes of ownership. The products of these enterprises are often referred to as "Thuringian Porcelain" generically. Obviously, the several factories can be discussed collectively.

GOTHA, KLOSTER VEILSDORF and VOLKSTEDT-RUDOLSTADT are the three principal factories of the nine, from the standpoint of artistic production. The paste materials of these enterprises were of good quality, but their modelers and decorators did not compare favorably with those of the great factories with which they competed. Collectors can find old pieces of some of these factories in German antique shops at reasonable prices.

GOTHA, which was established by Wilhelm von Rotberg in 1757, used a cream colored paste and translucent glaze. Rotberg leased the factory about 1782 to Christian Schulz, Johann Georg Gabel and Johann Adam Brehm, three of his leading artists. GOTHA produced items of excellent quality beginning around 1782, first in Rococo style and later in Louis XVI and Neo-Classical fashion (Fig. 168). Its vases, services, and useful items and cups and saucers were uniquely decorated with attractive single and multicolored landscapes and scenes, medals and coats of arms, characters, and black figure silhouettes often framed in gold and floral designs. This factory is reputed to have done the best decorating of any Thuringian establishment.

The GOTHA underglaze blue marks which were at first an R, then an R-g, and later an old-fashioned G, are shown in frames 16, 17 and 18, page 108.

KLOSTER VEILSDORF was established in 1760 with the patronage of Friedrich Wilhelm Eugen, Prince of Hildburghausen, who directed the factory for many years. It produced excellent quality porcelain first in creamy or greyish-white and later in pure white. Nikolaus Paul is reported to have served as *arcanist* from 1766 to 1768, but little is known of the factory's able artists. The Greiner family operated the factory between 1797 and 1832.

A great variety of good tableware and miscellaneous items composed the major production. Typical decorations of KLOSTER VEILSDORF are the large freely-painted purple, red and yellow flowers on thread-like stems. Flowers, trellises *chinoiseries*, landscapes and figure subjects were also employed on the various items. Honey states, "The early figures (which seldom bear a factory mark) include some strongly modelled characters from the Italian Comedy on mound bases, in the style of those made by Simon Feilner at Fürstenberg, with which they are sometimes confused, and Classical gods on square bases, the costumes often patterned with small red flowers." (Fig. 165).

The old factory mark is an underglaze blue monogram of the letters CV in varying forms and sometimes with a coat of arms as shown in frames 1, 2 and 4, page 109. After 1797 the three-leaf clover was used.

VOLKSTEDT-RUDOLSTADT was started by Georg Heinrich Macheleid around 1760 with the patronage of Johann Friedrich von Schwarzburg-Rudolstadt. It was leased to Christian Nonne during its best period between 1767 and 1797, after which it was sold to Prince Ernst Constantin von Hessen-Philippsthal who later sold it to the Greiners.

Penkala reports, "The paste used in the early days was very grey, but the quality was gradually improved until a fine white material was evolved. Up to 1800 production mainly comprised ordinary tableware and other articles in common use. These were of massive design and decorated in rococo style. In addition this factory produced a few services of superior quality, artistically decorated and beautifully, though sparingly, painted in delicate colors .In some instances a single colour only was employed, usually purple or red. Very beautiful vases (Fig. 163) in formal style were produced as well as figures in a somewhat heavy rococo style." Decorations also include small portraits in Rococo frames, landscapes and ornamental maps. In recent years, during which time Paul Scheurich and other able artists were employed, the factory has produced a variety of attractive tablewares, vases and figures (Fig. 171).

The early two-prong single or crossed pitchfork factory marks of various shapes and sizes are in underglaze blue. Beginning about 1800 a large R was used and new marks were adopted subsequently. The principal old and modern marks of VOLKSTEDT-RUDOLSTADT are shown in the bottom section of page 108 and in frame 19, page 113. The figures were usually unmarked.

The other six Thuringian Forest factories — WALLENDORF, LIMBACH, ILMENAU, GERA, GROSSBREITENBACH and RAUENSTEIN — confined their production primarily to tablewares and useful articles and have continued their operations with some interruptions to the present date. They improved their paste and glaze after some years of experience and made good quality utility products. Although they maintained an artistic staff, their general production was of commercial quality as they frankly admitted catering to a clientele of modest means. Many of their tablewares were painted in underglaze blue and a dull crimson. Some interesting and attractive pieces have been produced at different times which, as a matter of history and comparison, have considerable appeal to collectors. Each of these factories will be discussed briefly in the chronological order of their establishment.

WALLENDORF was founded in 1764 by Johann W. Hammann, who was soon joined by his two cousins Johann Gottfried and Gotthelf Greiner. The early porcelain was of comparatively poor quality, decorated in Rococo style. In later years some attractive services were made and decorated in a rather formal style. During the last quarter of the 18th century, a large amount of the *Geschirre* was decorated in blue. Pastoral and street scenes were also produced in monotones of purple, brown, black and occasionally in grey. WALLENDORF produced figures primarily of rural characters, musicians (Fig. 164) and other subjects which were interesting and attractive but of limited artistic value.

The marks are underglazed blue W's of variable sizes and shapes. Some of the early W's resemble MEISSEN crossed swords while others look like the WEGELY mark. WALLENDORF marks are shown in frames 11 ond 12, page 109.

LIMBACH was established in 1772 by Gotthelf Greiner who turned the factory over to his five sons in 1792. The first porcelain was yellowish but later evolved into a good quality white. The wholesale production of simple *Geschirre* was painted primarily in blue and purple. Some attractive vases were produced around 1780, but the best production of the factory was after 1800. LIMBACH figures of rustic subjects and small-town people were frequently decorated in interesting patterns of various colors (Fig. 169).

Marks of the factory are shown in frames 14 and 15, page 109. The combined letters LB or crossed L's were applied on the glaze in red, purple or black during the first years. Around 1787 an under-glaze blue clover leaf was employed. The clover leaf appeared in purple, black or gold later on.

ILMENAU was founded in 1777 by Christian Z. Gräbner, directed from 1782 by the Duke of Weimar and leased to Gotthelf Greiner in 1786. The porcelain at first was of inferior quality, but both the paste and glaze were later improved. Dinner and tea services and many other useful articles were made in the prevailing Neo-Classical fashion. Attractive monochrome cups (Fig. 167) and other souvenir items with Thuringian scenes in single or multicolors were produced. ILMENAU manu-factured some imitations of WEDGWOOD jasper-relief and portrait busts after 1800, which was the best period of the factory. Most of the existing items were made during the Empire and Biedermeier periods.

The factory marks which seem to have appeared about 1792 consist of the in-formal letter I or crossed J's and are shown in frames 16 and 17, page 109.

GERA, founded in 1779 by Prince Heinrich von Reuss, was purchased by the Greiner family soon thereafter. The paste and glaze were of greyish tone. The factory produced the usual line of useful porcelain and specialized in wood-grained wares which attracted considerable attention. The modeling was comparatively mediocre and many of the paintings were copies from other factories, the Neo-Classical style dominating. As special items the factory also produced loving cups, vases, pots and pitchers, cups and saucers with ruins, and landscapes and town scenes in natural colors (Fig. 166).

87

The G mark of GERA, frame 18, page 109, resembles the GOTZKOWSKY mark, frame 10, page 107, and G of GOTHA, frame 18, page 108. In addition to the old fashioned G mark, GERA products are also marked as shown in frames 19 and 20 on page 109. All marks are in underglazed blue.

GROSSBREITENBACH was founded in 1779 by Major von Hopfgarten but it was soon acquired by Gotthelf Greiner, who was often referred to as father of the Thuringian Forest potters. Little information is available on this relatively unimportant factory. Its products, as well as its clover-leaf marks, closely resemble LIMBACH of which it became a branch.

RAUENSTEIN was founded in 1783 by the Greiner Brothers with the consent of the Duke of Saxony-Meiningen. The factory produced a variety of services and useful items of ordinary quality, primarily in Neo-Classical fashion. The old mark was a crude blue R or R-n in various sizes as shown in frames 21 and 22, page 109, while the modern factory mark is shown in frame 11, page 112.

MINOR 18TH CENTURY FACTORIES
(1757 Onward)

Several other small factories, which are reported by some German writers and Honey or Penkala to have operated in the last half of the 18th century, should be mentioned as a matter of record. In chronological order of establishment, they include HANAU and BADEN-BADEN, about 1750; ELLWANGEN, about 1757; HÖXTER, about 1759; SCHNEY, about 1780; BLANKENHAIN, 1790; TETTAU, 1794; and EISENBERG, 1796. These factories closed after a few years of operation with the exception of TETTAU which still exists. Their products do not possess any outstanding characteristics or special qualities, but may be of historical interest to some collectors. Pieces from these small establishments are rarely seen in museums or antique shops; however, they can be purchased at reasonable prices as most dealers are not familiar with them. Marks of some of these factories are shown on page 109 while the others may be found in standard mark books.

FACTORIES OF THE 19TH AND 20TH CENTURIES

Germany and Austria and their former territories have a large number of porcelain factories which originated in the 19th and 20th centuries, some of which have established an international reputation for the manufacture of good quality utilitarian and decorative items.

Although little artistic or historical importance can be attached to products of the more modern establishments, amateurs and collectors, and especially dealers are usually interested in the role they have played in satisfying popular demand and stimulating general interest in porcelain.

The discovery of porcelain and the availability of suitable raw materials (Map, page 40) placed Germany early in the forefront of the great hard-paste porcelain industry, which is closely associated with her industrial and economic development. Emphasis has been on commercial production of as good quality as prices would justify. With the application of science and business methods, German porcelain products have competed successfully in the world markets for many decades. Although some of the porcelain factories in the large cities were destroyed or damaged during World War II, it was estimated that the porcelain plants as a whole suffered less than ten per cent damage. Practically all of them resumed full operation soon after the War and contributed materially to the export program in economic restoration.

Most of the 19th and 20th century factories, which approximate two hundred in number in the whole of Germany, are concentrated near the source of porcelain raw materials in the central and eastern part of Germany primarily – North Bavaria, Thuringia, Saxony and Silesia.

The products of these factories, some of which were established more than a hundred years ago, appear in abundance in many of the antique shops of Germany and other countries. Amateurs will be impressed with the best pieces of the well-known factories of SITZENDORF (Fig. 170), ROSENTHAL (Fig. 172), SCHUMANN, HUTSCHENREUTHER (Fig. 173) and HEINRICH (Fig. 174), for example. Indeed, their choicest products are attractive and tempting to the amateur. In addition, some of the leading decorators in Dresden and the manufacturers of Altwasser, Passau, Plaue, Potschappel, Rudolstadt, Selb and other cities have produced utilitarian and decorative porcelain of good quality. Despite the attractive appearance of many of the best modern pieces, they hardly compare in artistic quality with those produced by the master-modelers and decorators of the 18th century; and therefore have limited appeal to connoisseurs.

As previously stated, the famous old factories of MEISSEN, NYMPHENBURG, BERLIN and FÜRSTENBERG, the "Thuringian Forest" factories and several others which were established in the 18th century are still operating. They, along with the many 19th and 20th century establishments, are producing large quantities of porcelain in great variety for local use and export.

Because of territorial changes following World War I, a number of the Austrian manufactories were embraced in Czechoslovakia. MEISSEN, the old BERLIN enterprise and the Thuringian Forest factories of the 18th century, and perhaps a majority of the 19th and 20th century factories are located in the eastern part of Germany as shown on page 41.

The marks of the principal German porcelain factories of the 19th and 20th centuries appear in alphabetical order by location of establishments on pages 110 to 113. Marks of establishments in Austria and adjoining countries appear on page 115.

CHAPTER V

Suggestions for the Amateur

This chapter is written primarily for the information and encouragement of the beginner and not for the professional expert, advanced collector, or museum curator. It is intended for those with limited knowledge and experience — the amateur collector who desires to enjoy a delightful hobby but who is frustrated by the artistic and technical terminology used by most of the experts who have written so voluminously on the subject; the small dealer who does not specialize in porcelain but strives to handle good items; and last but not least, the homemaker who wishes to adorn the home with really charming, decorative and useful porcelain. Serious collectors and experienced dealers, however, may find many of these suggestions helpful in making selections.

COLLECTING OPPORTUNITIES

Anyone interested in collecting porcelain should realize in the beginning that this has been the hobby of countless people of varying circumstances in many parts of the world for more than two centuries. It is not restricted to people of wealth, the aesthetically trained or the sophisticated as so many persons are inclined to believe. It should also be remembered that even serious collectors were once amateurs and necessarily had to learn from study, observation and experience. Consequently, almost anyone who develops an interest in porcelain and has good taste, a fairly good eye, and is willing to do a reasonable amount of studying, consulting, and observing should soon be able to make creditable selections. Timidity will disappear with study and experience, and the amateur will be able to discuss the history, quality and marks of porcelain with increasing confidence and authority.

At the same time amateurs will begin to realize that porcelain, which is only one segment of the whole field of ceramics, is so extensive in itself that it is desirable, if not necessary, to concentrate their studies and collecting to some particular aspect of this broad field. For example, some may desire to collect tea-pots of all shapes, sources and ages, while others may collect almost anything of a certain factory or mark, a specific period, or a definite style, color or composition. The opportunities for collecting porcelain are almost unlimited.

BASIC PROCEDURES IN COLLECTING

There is no direct or sure method for the average person to follow in achieving expert proficiency in a short time; but like all other hobbies or games, there are some basic criteria and practices which will be found helpful. The beginner should observe the following:

1. *Acquire standard books* and magazines in the general field of your hobby and add more specialized ones as your interest and taste develop. Well chosen books, like properly selected porcelain, are a good investment. Most factories distribute books which give an historical account of their development and provide illustrations of their better pieces. Museums can supply at a nominal charge illustrated booklets of their porcelain collections.

2. *Study the photographs* of famous pieces as it is impossible to see all of the originals. Glossy pictures of artistic porcelain can be purchased from museums or photographic agencies at very moderate prices and will add materially to your reference library. Most public libraries have porcelain books which contain black-and-white as well as colored pictures of outstanding pieces. One may find it helpful and most interesting to have pieces of his own collection photographed in color for the screen, and in black-and-white for mounting. Illustrated auction catalogs, as listed on page 226 and discussed on page 26, are also helpful.

92

3. *Visit shops, exhibits, auctions, museums and private collections* and learn to distinguish the "good" and the "bad" by cultivating a "feeling" for porcelain. The habit of close critical observation must be developed. Acquaintance and familiarity by sight and touch are necessary to complement the knowledge gained by reading and conversing.

4. *Study the porcelain marks.* Although they are often an unreliable clue to identification, a working knowledge of them is necessary in order to identify genuine pieces as well as falsifications. The subject of marks is discussed at some length in the last part of this chapter.

5. *Buy a few representative authentic pieces* from unquestionable sources and use them as a basis for comparison with the items you contemplate purchasing. Genuine pieces will expose fakes, as the style, decoration, and general quality will show marked contrasts.

6. *Cultivate an acquaintance* or friendship with persons who are interested and experienced in porcelain — collectors, dealers, exhibitors and, if possible, ceramics specialists in museums. They are usually willing to advise and some may take pride in actually assisting, which will save the beginner many avoidable mistakes. Ceramics curators in museums are usually unbiased and well qualified and, as public employees, are willing to answer your questions either by interview or correspondence. Some museums, however, make it a rule not to give information on objects which are in the process of sale, as advice under such circumstances may lead to misunderstandings with dealers.

INSPECTING AND APPRAISING

Certain techniques will be found helpful in handling a piece of porcelain to determine its manufacture, age, and artistic and physical quality.

In picking up an item be careful but don't be timid. Confidence and skill in handling will develop with experience. Use both hands while making a thorough inspection. Never hold a figure by the arm or an appendage. Pick it up by placing the fingers of one hand securely around the head and shoulders and then support the base with the other hand. Avoid holding cups, vases, tea-pots and such items by their handles, spouts or other weak places. Grasp the piece by placing all fingers of one hand except the thumb in the hollow part, then support the bottom with the other hand. When an item consists of more than one part inspect the pieces separately. For example, the top of a tea-pot should be removed before handling the pot.

Assuming that the amateur has gained a working knowledge on the subject of porcelain through a program of study, observation and inspection, the responsibility of intelligent shopping now rests upon his own shoulders. The observation of at least five factors will be found helpful in judging the quality and genuineness of a piece of porcelain:

1. *The factory mark* is a good clue but not a guarantee of the origin of a piece of porcelain. Marks are generally reliable but some pieces are falsely marked, others are copies, while some have no marks at all. The discussion on pages 101 through 105 and the illustrations on pages 106 to 116 give many details on the use and reliability of factory marks.

2. *The body or paste* of the material reveals its texture, degree of whiteness, translucency and general physical quality. A good paste is fine-grained, uniform in color, and reasonably free from defects. Early MEISSEN and VIENNA and some other old porcelains have a green tone, are irregular in texture and translucency, and often possess light spots or "moons" when viewed by transmitted light, as explained on page 43. Collectors rely upon these spots to determine antiquity as most MEISSEN and VIENNA in the first half of the 18th century and early pieces of some other factories possess "moons" of varying sizes and shapes. To determine whether the item is pottery or porcelain and furthermore whether it is hard-paste or soft-paste, one should tap it with the fingers or a pencil for sound, or scratch the unglazed part under the bottom (foot rim) slightly with a knife or file to ascertain texture. Hard-paste porcelain will have a bell-like or metallic ring, and the material will be difficult to scratch. By placing the fingers behind a plate or similar object and holding it before a bright light, it is possible to determine whether or not it is porcelain by its translucency. A piece of good 19th or 20th century porcelain usually shows an even translucency varying, of course, according to its composition and thickness. The various kinds of porcelain and other ceramics are described on pages 35, 37, 38 and in the Glossary.

3. *The glaze* should be scrutinized for transparency, thickness and reflective luster. Turn the piece over and around in all directions to determine the reflections. If the glaze is dull or scratched and is of varying texture or thickness, the value of the piece is affected accordingly. Biscuit porcelain which has been fired but unglazed is easily detected by its marble-like appearance (Figs. 100 and 111).

4. *The form and contour* of the item is also an important factor in determining the age and artistic value of a piece, as explained on pages 20 to 24. Many old porcelain pieces have been copied in recent years, but an old form with a characteristic decoration of the same period, further associated with an old factory mark, make a combination of factors which practically guarantees antiquity.

5. *The decoration* is a decisive factor in determining the age and final quality of the piece. The pattern design, subject of the painting, combination of colors and degree of gilding affect the beauty and value of the piece and in considerable measure determine the age. The process of underglaze and on-glaze decoration is described on pages 36 and 37.

The techniques of inspection vary somewhat among the connoisseurs, but as a rule they make the same basic observations. An outstanding European museum ceramics curator summed up his method of appraising a porcelain item by saying, "I first look for the mark at the bottom of a piece. If a mark exists, I know which factory is supposed to be responsible for the item. For example, I see a MEISSEN mark, so I now look at the general composition of the piece and the foot rim to determine whether or not they are characteristic of the factory and period indicated by the mark. Then I want to know whether mass and glaze are old or new. I conclude in this case, for instance, that mass and glaze are old. Now I look at the decoration or painting. This is important as many old pieces have been bought or smuggled from the dealers and brought to forgers for repainting or remarking. Then I check the decoration as there are various patterns or styles of particular periods which could be used in decorating. Next I ask myself whether the decoration goes with the form, mass and mark of this MEISSEN piece, since many of the forgers of MEISSEN porcelain who lived principally in near-by Dresden were able to copy the most delicate color arrangements from the originals in the Dresden museums and sometimes even had the opportunity of borrowing them. Finally, because of my long experience with this kind of material, I conclude that all

95

characteristics are in harmony and that the piece is genuine MEISSEN and old. In all instances the item must sell itself and convince me of its originality, age and general merit. I find there is no other recipe."

FORGERIES AND RESTORATIONS

Buyers are always confronted with the problem of determining genuine pieces of old porcelain from later forgeries or falsifications. They must also be able to detect defects and repairs which are often hidden by masterful restorations. Numerous individuals and establishments have operated since the 18th century and continue to specialize in producing pieces to order. They can copy almost any piece expertly in form, size, color and marks. There are also repair shops which can restore damaged pieces so cleverly that it is difficult to discover the defects. All collectors have been deceived at one time or another and amateurs can certainly expect to make mistakes. However, there are certain standards which are helpful in determining falsifications and restorations. A magnifying glass and sometimes an ultraviolet lamp are useful in making the necessary inspection.

1. *Scratches under the painting* are positive proof of forgery as they reveal that the piece was painted considerably later than its manufacture. In such a case the surface of the porcelain had become worn and scratched through ordinary use and handling. To increase its value by decorating at a later date the artist necessarily applied the paintings over the scratches which definitely reveal falsification.

2. *Artificial scratches* are sometimes applied on comparatively new white or painted porcelain pieces to suggest antiquity. One must learn the differences between traces of wear—scratches from natural daily use—and those which have been applied artificially by rubbing with emery paper or steel wool, for example. The scratches from normal use appear irregularly on the exposed parts of the items, while those which are counterfeited can be recognized by their uniformity and fresh appearance.

3. *The form and color of painting* is always a decisive factor in judging the authenticity of a piece. Forgers are very clever, but they often commit errors by applying inappropriate colors on a piece of certain age or design, and frequently

the quality of their brushwork is off-type. Falsifications are generally noticeable by their severity and lack of elegance in style and color. Sometimes colors are employed which were not used in the 18th century, for instance, maroon and yellowish green made from chromium. Often a design of a later period is applied on an old piece or an old-style painting is used on a new form. The gold decoration may also prove the genuineness of an old piece of good quality. Old gilding is usually applied in a heavy layer and has a warm vigorous golden shine, whereas falsifications make a faint and new impression.

4. *The color of the eyes* of a figure may be helpful in determining its age. Practically all figures of the 18th century have brown eyes. The blue-eyed figures appeared later. Of course, many brown-eyed figures were made in the 19th and 20th centuries along with the blue, and some are difficult to distinguish from the originals of earlier times.

5. *Breakage is prevalent* and many pieces of old porcelain have been slightly or seriously damaged. Often the damaged pieces have been repaired (restored), so it is necessary to scrutinize every item carefully. The fingers, arms, feet, necks and other appendages of figures are the places most likely to be damaged. Handles, spouts, feet, stems, edges and bases of tablewares are the most susceptible parts to breakage. If you suspect that the piece has been restored, use your magnifying glass and an ultraviolet lamp, if necessary. Thump the item with the fingernails to see that it has the clear metallic ring of a complete piece. The difference in color, texture and touch usually reveals repair work. Another way to detect repairs is by smell as the odor of lacquer lingers for a long time. If still in doubt as to a possible restoration, ask the dealer for permission to submerge the piece in warm water for a few minutes as broken parts will probably separate from the main body.

6. *Mismatched pieces are common*, so it is important to see that the parts of an item and the pieces of a set match in quality of material, form, and in decoration. Frequently old tea-pots and similar containers have tops of a different age or style. This can usually be determined by the comparatively fresh white color of a later lid or by the decoration which may vary in style or colors. Old cups and saucers, vases, trays, and tea and desk sets are often mismatched and not detected until the purchase is made. Every piece should be laid out and matched piece by piece to determine if there are any discrepancies.

One should realize, however, that restoration is not falsification although repairs are sometimes intended to deceive. The older and more delicate an item is the more likely it is to be damaged whether it be porcelain, glass, wood, fibre, metal or some other material. Consequently, many old art pieces, especially those of porcelain, have been damaged through natural wear or accidental breakage. It may be a matter of opinion or taste as well as expediency as to how and to what extent a broken piece should be restored. Obviously broken-off parts are usually replaced rather than left in a drawer. Likewise, a collector or museum may prefer a good imitation lid to complete a precious old tea-pot than to have no lid at all. Most museums and art shops employ expert repairers and spend much time and money in maintaining and restoring porcelain and other pieces of art. Certainly this is not considered forgery. However, restored pieces have less artistic and material value than undamaged ones, and the amateur should be prepared to protect his interest in making selections.

THINGS NOT TO DO

As stated, there are no fixed formulae or set of rules that meet all circumstances. Ideas and taste vary considerably with individuals but the basic principles remain. The prevailing desire on the part of an amateur is to develop good taste and appreciation for both antique and modern porcelain. As there are certain things *to do* in selecting porcelain, there are certain things *not to do*. In order to avoid as many mistakes as possible, the following *don'ts* are submitted for the consideration of those with limited experience.

1. *Don't* buy anything for your permanent collection which is distasteful as you have to live with it. It should be remembered that beauty is the first criterion of every good collector.

2. *Don't* purchase an article simply because it has the mark of a good factory. Inferior porcelain is still bad regardless of the mark. On the other hand, there are many unmarked pieces of superior quality.

3. *Don't* acquire old pieces for the sake of their age, as antiquity adds little to the worth of an article unless it has historical or artistic value.

4. *Don't* buy pieces which are materially damaged or poorly mended because they may be reasonably priced. The cost of repairing may increase the final price to that of a perfect piece, and you still have a restored one.

5. *Don't* buy pieces under poorly lighted conditions unless you are willing to be deceived. Bright daylight is preferable as the true color as well as the defects are visible only under ideal light.

6. *Don't* rush or buy when in doubt. The dealer will usually reserve the piece for a short time thereby allowing you to reflect and compare before making the final decision.

BUYER-DEALER RELATIONS

The amateur will soon learn that it pays to make a round of visits to all antique shops periodically. Good pieces come and go and one never knows where or when he will run across a treasure.

As a rule, the large well established dealers are reliable and know their business, handle only worthwhile articles and charge a fair price without much leeway for bargaining. However, some are collectors themselves and do not offer the choice pieces for sale except to their favored clients. On the other hand, many of the small shops buy or sell almost anything, regardless of quality, for a small profit or commission. They occasionally buy good pieces cheaply and are willing to sell them for quick gain, not knowing or particularly caring what they are handling. It is in such shops that many valuable acquisitions are made.

When dealers become familiar with your interest and taste, they may be very helpful in locating and setting aside items which they believe will interest you. They are anxious to cultivate satisfied clients; so mutual understanding and confidence will develop a business relationship which will be advantageous to both the buyer and the dealer.

It is only fair to warn the amateur that good pieces of old porcelain from favorite factories command comparatively high prices. This is particularly true of figures which are often sold for fantastic sums. No attempt will be made to indicate or compare costs as they are so variable from country to country and among cities of

99

a single country. The season of the year, the general price level, and whether purchased privately, in a shop or on auction are a few of the other factors which determine price. Artistic porcelain, like most luxury items, is very sensitive to general economic conditions. During financial depressions the sales value may drop to less than half of the normal price, while during inflationary periods the prices rise greatly out of proportion to their real value. One should realize, however, that old artistic porcelain is very scarce and becoming more so and as time goes on may be expected to increase in value. As a rule, carefully selected porcelain bought at a fair price is considered a good investment. Many collectors purchase cautiously. By careful and industrious shopping, they try to acquire pieces which are at least worth the price paid.

Considering all factors, it is advantageous to shop for porcelain of a desired source in the country where it was produced, since indigenous items are usually available in greater variety of form, age, and price. This is particularly true in Germany where antique shops appear content in stocking German porcelain almost exclusively; whereas shops of other European countries ordinarily have a more cosmopolitan selection. Porcelain of a certain factory is usually more abundant in the locality where it was produced, as one would suspect. For example, BERLIN wares of all periods are generally available in most Berlin shops, but rarely seen in remote parts of Germany or surrounding countries.

Amateurs will learn that trends in porcelain collecting vary from time to time according to prevailing vogues. Collectors have their individual ideas and tastes, but are frequently influenced by the fashion and spirit of the times. Consequently, many are trying to collect the same things at the same time. Most collectors are now striving to acquire good quality 18th century painted pieces which were produced during the early operation of a factory. Because of the competition for early painted items, prices are almost prohibitive for anyone of moderate means. On the other hand, many artistic pieces, especially white porcelain of the 18th century and interesting pieces of the Biedermeier period are going unnoticed at reasonable prices. Careful selections of items "not in vogue" may result in an interesting collection well worth the investment. However, an amateur who "swims against the current" may acquire a collection which will have limited artistic appeal and material value to others.

THE MARKS

Something should be said here on the general subject of porcelain marks since they are sure to confuse the amateur as much as they continue to perplex the seasoned collector. The lists of German and Austrian marks which are presented on pages 106 through 116 were specially designed and arranged for the convenience of the amateur and are believed to be as up-to-date and reliable as any existing set.

For the information of the reader, it should be stated that historical and scientific evidence is inadequate to prepare an accurate and complete set of all marks for the various periods of the several important factories. Although factory marks were designed for some purpose or reason, in most instances there was little foresight and planning in establishing a systematic series of marks which would significantly typify the various styles or periods of the factory. Consequently, marks were more or less created and modified according to the press of circumstances and the whims of factory patrons, directors and modelers.

The original list of marks was prepared decades ago and subsequent writers on this subject have copied and perpetuated many of the mistakes. Numerous mark books have been prepared by courageous individuals in the meantime, but none is completely reliable for the reasons stated above and for the fact that the subject is so broad that it is practically impossible for one critic to give the whole array of marks a comparative scientific appraisal and presentation. Even if all marks in the books were accurate, the amateur and collector would still have the problem of deciding whether the mark on the piece is a correct factory mark or a falsification.

Regardless of the lack of completeness and accuracy of available mark books and the prevalence of falsified marks on occasional pieces, the amateur will soon learn to recognize the principal marks and suspect the false ones. He will find a standard set of marks reasonably reliable and most helpful in identifying the manufacturer and obtaining other pertinent information on the piece.

The following are a few peculiarities and generalizations concerning marks:

1. In speaking of "marks," the reference is primarily to the factory mark which is the symbol or trade mark of a certain establishment. For example the crossed swords of MEISSEN, the ribbon-shield of VIENNA, the wheel of HÖCHST, the shield of NYMPHENBURG and the scepter of BERLIN are well known.

101

2. A majority of the factory marks are hand-drawn or impressed (stamped) in blue in the white porcelain material before it is fired and glazed, while a few appear in other colors. In some cases marks are stamped or drawn on the glaze in various colors — blue, red and gold — and are fused with the glaze during a later firing. As a rule, a certain factory will use the same color and method of marking, but the design of the mark may change somewhat with the period, management, or for some other reason. Most factories place their marks on the bottom of pieces. NYMPHENBURG, however, frequently exposes its marks on the side or pedestal of an item, and some of the old MEISSEN figures are marked on the back of their pedestals, and tablewares may be marked inside.

3. In addition to the factory mark there may be accessory marks such as initials or numbers — either incised, impressed or in colors. Incised marks (hand-drawn with a pointed instrument in the unfired material usually give technical information on the piece or its composition and are not intended for the workmen's glory. Impressed (stamped) and painted numbers or symbols may refer to the year of manufacture, the model or inventory list, the style or pattern, the composition of the material, to a workman, or may have some other significance according to the customs of the factory concerned.

As a rule, artists did not initial or sign their models or decorations as such was discouraged by the old establishments. Painters occasionally added their initials for purposes of record, but great artists like Bustelli and Melchior rarely signed their pieces. Signatures always cause speculation as to whether the item is out-standing, a falsification or one decorated privately.

4. Since many of the old marks were made by hand, those of a specific period for a certain factory may vary somewhat in design and size according to the individuality of the workman and the size of the piece. Handmade marks are often drawn larger on large pieces. Records indicate that many old pieces of MEISSEN were marked by 14-year-old apprentices who could scarcely read or write, which may account for the great variability of the old marks of this factory.

5. A small proportion of the best old pieces as well as some of the later ones have no marks of any kind. There are several explanations for the absence of a mark. Some of the pieces were left unmarked by accident, and several factories sold unmarked white pieces for private decoration. A legend, believed to be a fable,

circulates among some European dealers that Napoleon, as Emperor, ordered all factories either to use his initial and crown as a mark or omit the mark altogether. Consequently, some unmarked pieces, often of modern appearance, are claimed to have been made during the Empire period, from about 1804 to 1814.

6. It has been observed that falsifications of some German marks are about as prevalent outside of Germany as within, since boundaries and distance from the source of production work in favor of counterfeiters. This is not necessarily true of the very first forgeries, many of which were done in or near Dresden.

7. Practically all MEISSEN products have been marked from about 1725 to the present date as shown on page 106. In the case of figures and groups produced from around 1735 to 1745, the crossed swords mark which was applied under the unglazed base was frequently dimmed or obliterated in the firing process. Consequently, the practice of applying a smaller mark on the back side of figure bases was adopted somewhere around 1740 to 1745.

8. Many American and some European novices are confused between MEISSEN and "Dresden" marks and what they mean. The original MEISSEN factory, which is now a State factory, is situated in the town of Meissen which is only 14 miles from the large city of Dresden, the capital of Saxony. Consequently, MEISSEN is often referred to as "Dresden" and vice versa by English-speaking peoples and in English-language books, but there is a definite distinction.

Porcelain is not manufactured in Dresden, but several factories are situated near by and a large number some distance away. Enormous quantities of white porcelain are bought by Dresden firms only for decorating, marking and reselling throughout the world as "Dresden China." Few of the Dresden decorating establishments have produced artistic porcelain, but all enjoy the prestige of their location and the privilege of connecting the famous word "Dresden" with their trade mark. "Dresden," therefore, is a generic term which applies to any and every piece of porcelain which is hand or mechanically painted in the city or environs. On the other hand, there is only one State MEISSEN factory, and that is the one started by August the Strong at MEISSEN in 1710.

9. One often sees a factory mark with one, two, three, or even four mechanical cuts or strikes engraved across the mark. Such strikes, sometimes erroneously referred to as "connoisseur marks," usually denote the degree of defectiveness —

the more cuts or strikes the poorer the quality. MEISSEN, for instance, started grading and marking its products early in the 19th century. Items of incontestable quality have no slashes across the crossed swords factory mark at all. Pieces with minor defects are graded as second quality and receive two emery-wheel slashes across the mark as shown in the lower left frame on page 116. Items with more serious defects are of third quality, and are slashed three times; while four strikes indicate that the piece is inferior in quality and not sold to the public directly, but disposed of to the workmen of the factory at a very low price. In general, MEISSEN does not sell plain white figures or other wares, excepting some of second and third quality. In such cases the usual two or three slashes are made across the mark and another cut is added on the side running parallel with the axis of the swords. The latter stroke indicates that the piece was sold unpainted; and if such piece is retailed in painted condition, it can be assumed that the decoration was added later outside the factory. The practice of the old MEISSEN factory outlined above applies only to porcelain made after 1800. Before that date, one cut usually indicated that the piece was sold in an undecorated state as shown in the lower left-hand corner of page 116.

Several other factories, including BERLIN and FÜRSTENBERG, use a somewhat similar method of marking their wares of inferior quality. Such a system of identifying defective pieces is designed to protect the buyer as well as the reputation of the factory for quality production.

10. In a number of instances porcelain factories have accidentally or deliberately adopted marks which were very similar or almost identical to the established marks of the famous old factories. For example, the crossed swords of MEISSEN with slight variations have been used by several old and modern German and non-German factories, as can be seen in the accompanying set of marks and especially on page 116. Likewise the KPM or scepter mark of BERLIN, the wheel mark of HÖCHST and the double-C mark of LUDWIGSBURG have also been imitated as can be seen in the section on German marks and on page 116. With study and experience one should not find it difficult to detect the difference between imitated and falsified marks, as well as falsified pieces.

EXPLANATION OF THE MARKS

The abbreviated lists of German and Austrian porcelain marks which appear on the following pages were especially prepared and arranged with the assistance and counsel of several museum curators, collectors, dealers and manufacturers. They are as reliable as the available sources of information and should be helpful to the amateur, collector, and dealer. ❧ The marks are hand drawn, in actual size as far as practical, and in many cases were sketched from typical pieces of porcelain of the various factories. Most of the marks are blue under the glaze, but some are of other colors either under or on the glaze; and a few are impressed as indicated. Additional information on the marks of the several factories can be found at the end of the discussion of each establishment in Chapters III and IV. ❧ Marks of the 18th century factories are arranged chronologically while those of 98 prominent establishments which were founded in the 19th and 20th centuries are arranged alphabetically by location primarily for the benefit of dealers. The numbers appearing in the upper left-hand corner of the small individual frames on each page of marks are included for the convenience of making cross-references from the text. ❧ Although the marks contained herein are designed to serve collectors, dealers and amateurs in the most convenient fashion, it is realized that rare marks, painter and modeler marks, date and catalog serial numbers and other unusual information must necessarily be sought in the voluminous books and special mark catalogs prepared by the manufacturers.

GERMAN PORCELAIN

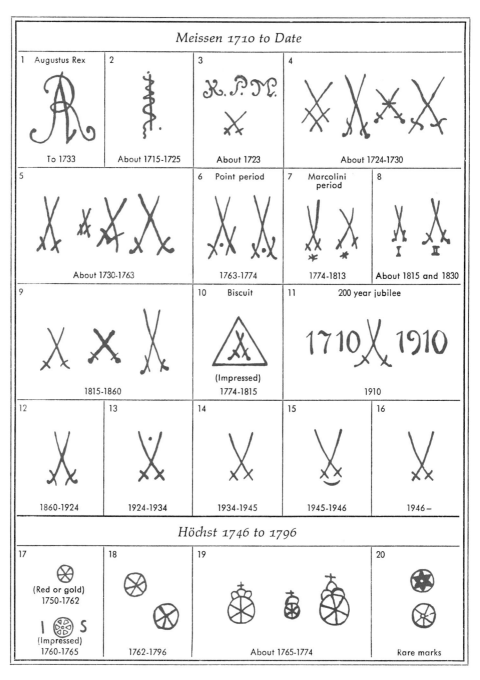

Meissen 1710 to Date

1 Augustus Rex — To 1733

2 About 1715-1725

3 About 1723

4 About 1724-1730

5 About 1730-1763

6 Point period — 1763-1774

7 Marcolini period — 1774-1813

8 About 1815 and 1830

9 1815-1860

10 Biscuit — (Impressed) 1774-1815

11 200 year jubilee — 1910

12 1860-1924

13 1924-1934

14 1934-1945

15 1945-1946

16 1946 –

Höchst 1746 to 1796

17 (Red or gold) 1750-1762 — (Impressed) 1760-1765

18 1762-1796

19 About 1765-1774

20 Rare marks

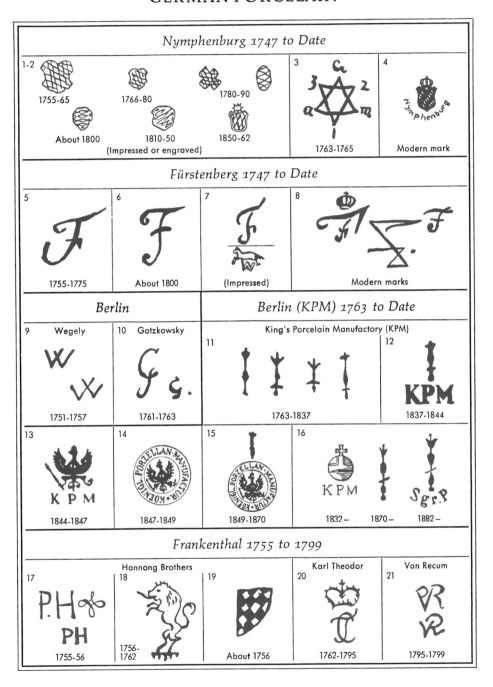

Nymphenburg 1747 to Date

1-2
1755-65
1766-80
1780-90
About 1800
1810-50 (Impressed or engraved)
1850-62

3
1763-1765

4
Modern mark

Fürstenberg 1747 to Date

5
1755-1775

6
About 1800

7
(Impressed)

8
Modern marks

Berlin

Berlin (KPM) 1763 to Date

King's Porcelain Manufactory (KPM)

9 Wegely
1751-1757

10 Gotzkowsky
1761-1763

11
1763-1837

12
1837-1844

13
1844-1847

14
1847-1849

15
1849-1870

16
1832—   1870—   1882—

Frankenthal 1755 to 1799

17
P.H
PH
1755-56

Hannong Brothers
18
1756-1762

19
About 1756

Karl Theodor
20
1762-1795

Van Recum
21
1795-1799

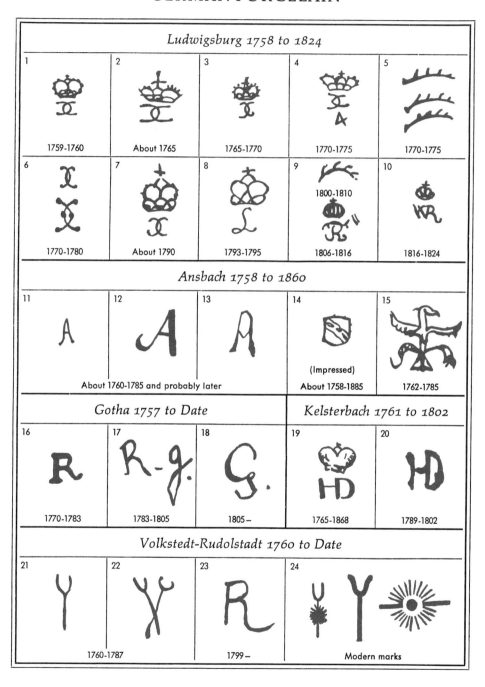

Ludwigsburg 1758 to 1824

1 — 1759-1760	2 — About 1765	3 — 1765-1770	4 — 1770-1775	5 — 1770-1775
6 — 1770-1780	7 — About 1790	8 — 1793-1795	9 — 1800-1810 / 1806-1816	10 — 1816-1824

Ansbach 1758 to 1860

11	12	13	14 (Impressed) About 1758-1885	15 — 1762-1785
	About 1760-1785 and probably later			

Gotha 1757 to Date | **Kelsterbach 1761 to 1802**

16 — 1770-1783	17 — 1783-1805	18 — 1805—	19 — 1765-1868	20 — 1789-1802

Volkstedt-Rudolstadt 1760 to Date

21	22 — 1760-1787	23 — 1799—	24 — Modern marks

GERMAN PORCELAIN

Kloster Veilsdorf 1760 to Date				Ottweiler
1 About 1775	2 C V.	3 1797 –	4 1760-1797	5 .N.S. 1763-1775

Fulda 1764 to 1790			Kassel 1766-88	Gutenbrunn
6 1765-1788	7 + 1765-1780	8 1765-1788	9 HC 1770-1788	10 B. 1767-1775

Wallendorf 1764 to Date		Würzburg	Limbach 1772 to Date	
11 W W.	12 1764-1788 and later	13 C . G W (Impresseu) W 1775-1780	14 (Purple or red) 1772-1787	15 (Black) 1787 –

Ilmenau 1777 to Date		Gera 1779 to Date		
16 i	17	18 G.G.	19 C G	20 Gera

Rauenstein 1783 to Date		Tettau 1794	Eisenberg 1796 to Date	
21 R R	22 R - n . R - n	23 T.	24 E.	25 SPM

GERMAN PORCELAIN 19 AND 20 CENTURIES

Altwasser		Arzberg	Bock-Wallendorf	Buchsbad
1	2	3	4	5
C.T.		*Schumann*		
Tielsch & Co.		C. Schumann	Fasold & Stauch	

Dresden (Decorators)

6	7	8	9	10
Dresden		*Dresden*	*A*	
	A. Hamann	Donath & Co.	Helena Wolfsohn	

Dresden (Decorators)

11	12	13	14	15
DRESDEN	*Dresden*	Dresden	*dresden.*	R.P.M
F. Junkersdorf	Franziska Hirsch		A. Lamm	H. Richter
16	17	18	19	20
Dresden	*Dresden*	*Dresden*	Dresden.	DRESDEN.
	K. R. Klemm		Heufel & Co.	

Elgersburg	Eisenberg		Fraureuth	Freienwaldau
21	22	23	24	25
		P R M E	SAXONY	H S
Eichhorn	Kalk	Reinecke		H. Schmidt

110

GERMAN PORCELAIN 19 AND 20 CENTURIES

Gehren	Graefenroda	Graefenthal	Gross-Breitenbach	Hohenberg
1	2	3	4	5
	Dornheim	C. Schneider	Bühl & Söhne	C. M. Hutschenreuther

Hüttensteinach		Ilmenau		
6 (Hirsch)	7	8	9	10
	Schönau, Swaine & Co.	Galluba & Hoffman		Metzler & Ortloff

Königszelt	Kolmar	Koppelsdorf	Lettin	Lichte
11	12	13	14	15
A.R.		A. Marseille	H. Baensch	Heubach

Limbach		Magdeburg	Margarethen-hütte	Marktredwitz
16	17	18	19	20
Porzellanfabrik Limbach		Buckau		

Meissen (City)			Neuhaldensleben	
21	22	23	24	25
	C. Teichert	Ernst Teichert	Sauer	

Neuhaus	Neu-Schmiedefeld	Nieder-Salzbrunn	Oberhohndorf	Oberkotzau
1	2	3	4 F. Kaester	5
Kämpfe & List	G. Korn			Greiner & Herda

Passau		Planken-hammer	Plaue	
6 Volkstedt		7	8	
(Copied marks)	(Original)		Plaue	
Dressel, Kister & Co.			Schierholz & Sohn	

Poessneck	Potschappel		Rauenstein
9	10		11
Conta & Boehme	Sächsische Porzellanfabrik (Carl Thieme)		Greiner

Rudolstadt	Saargemünd	Schaala	Scheibe
12	13	14	15 K.P.M
E. Bohne		H. Voigt	A. Kister

Schney	Schönwald	Schorndorf
16	17	18
E. Liebmann	Müller	Württembergische Porzellan Manufaktur

Selb				
1 Rosenthal	2 R.C.	3 Rosenthal	4 Hutschenreuther Selb. L.H.S	5 JHR Hutschenreuther Selb
	Rosenthal & Co.		L. Hutschenreuther	

Selb			Sitzendorf	Sorau
6 H&C SELB BAVARIA GERMANY Heinrich	7 K&A Krautheim SELB BAVARIA	8 PAUL MÜLLER SELB	9	10 P S P S
Heinrich & Co.	Krautheim	P. Müller	A. Voigt	

Suhl	Tiefenfurth		Tillowitz	Tirschenreuth
11 SCHLEGELMILCH 1861 SUHL	12 S S	13 TPM	14	15 P2. BAVARIA
	P. Donath			

Unterweissbach	Volkstedt (Rudolstadt)			
16	17	18 Aelteste Volkstedt		19
Schwarzburger	Ackermann		Eckert & Co.	

Waldenburg		Waldsassen	Wallendorf	Weingarten
20 KPM K.P.M.	21 KPM K WPM K. Krister	22 B P W C PW B C WALDSASSEN	23 W W	24 RK.W
			Kaempfe	

AUSTRIAN PORCELAIN

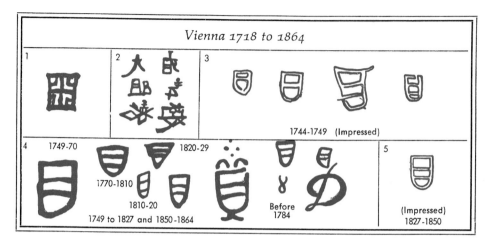

Vienna 1718 to 1864

1	2	3	
		1744-1749 (Impressed)	

4 1749-70	1820-29	5
1770-1810		
1810-20	Before 1784	(Impressed) 1827-1850
1749 to 1827 and 1850-1864		

CZECHOSLOVAKIAN PORCELAIN

Schlaggenwald	Klosterle 1793	Prague 1793 to Date	
6 1792	7	8	9
		(Impressed)	

Giesshubel 1802 to Date		Pirkenhammer 1803 to Date		
10	11	12	13	14
			(Impressed)	

Tannova	Dallwitz	Elbogen 1815 to Date		
15 1813	16 1802	17	18	19
				Modern mark

114

S. E. EUROPEAN PORCELAIN 19 AND 20 CENTURIES

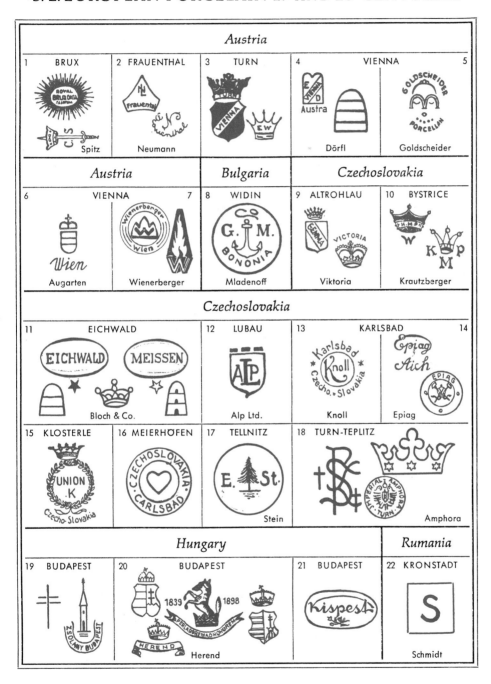

Austria

| 1 BRUX — Spitz | 2 FRAUENTHAL — Neumann | 3 TURN | 4 VIENNA — Dörfl | 5 — Goldscheider |

Austria | **Bulgaria** | **Czechoslovakia**

| 6 VIENNA — Augarten | 7 — Wienerberger | 8 WIDIN — Mladenoff | 9 ALTROHLAU — Viktoria | 10 BYSTRICE — Krautzberger |

Czechoslovakia

| 11 EICHWALD — Bloch & Co. | 12 LUBAU — Alp Ltd. | 13 KARLSBAD — Knoll | 14 — Epiag |

| 15 KLOSTERLE | 16 MEIERHÖFEN | 17 TELLNITZ — Stein | 18 TURN-TEPLITZ — Amphora |

Hungary | **Rumania**

| 19 BUDAPEST | 20 BUDAPEST — Herend | 21 BUDAPEST | 22 KRONSTADT — Schmidt |

SIMILAR MARKS

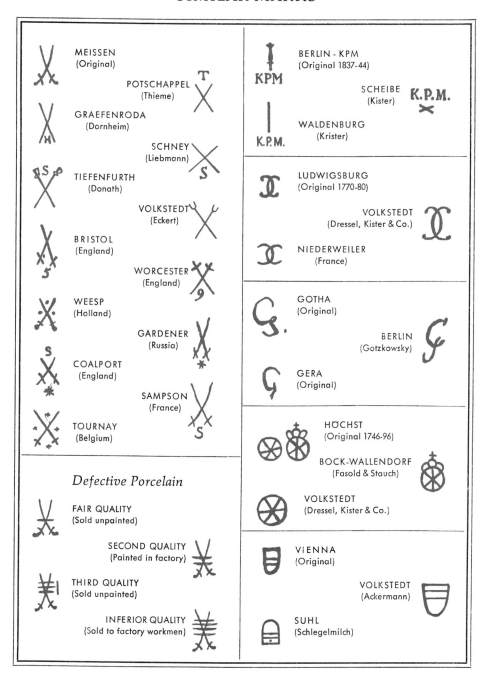

MEISSEN
(Original)

POTSCHAPPEL
(Thieme)

GRAEFENRODA
(Dornheim)

SCHNEY
(Liebmann)

TIEFENFURTH
(Donath)

VOLKSTEDT
(Eckert)

BRISTOL
(England)

WORCESTER
(England)

WEESP
(Holland)

GARDENER
(Russia)

COALPORT
(England)

SAMPSON
(France)

TOURNAY
(Belgium)

Defective Porcelain

FAIR QUALITY
(Sold unpainted)

SECOND QUALITY
(Painted in factory)

THIRD QUALITY
(Sold unpainted)

INFERIOR QUALITY
(Sold to factory workmen)

BERLIN - KPM
(Original 1837-44)

SCHEIBE
(Kister)

WALDENBURG
(Krister)

LUDWIGSBURG
(Original 1770-80)

VOLKSTEDT
(Dressel, Kister & Co.)

NIEDERWEILER
(France)

GOTHA
(Original)

BERLIN
(Gotzkowsky)

GERA
(Original)

HÖCHST
(Original 1746-96)

BOCK-WALLENDORF
(Fasold & Stauch)

VOLKSTEDT
(Dressel, Kister & Co.)

VIENNA
(Original)

VOLKSTEDT
(Ackermann)

SUHL
(Schlegelmilch)

EXPLANATION OF THE REPRODUCTIONS

The 174 reproductions of porcelain appearing on the following pages were graciously supplied by the 23 museums of nine countries which are listed on page 225, and from 18 private sources. Representative pieces of artistic porcelains from 26 factories are embraced in what may be the most cosmopolitan group of German and Austrian porcelain pictures appearing in any text. The selection and arrangement of photographs are designed to stimulate the interest of readers and give them the most complete pictorial information possible within the limitations of this publication. Although a majority of the items shown are outstanding museum pieces, a liberal quantity of "collectors items" which have been authenticated by experts are purposely included to depict good-quality artistic porcelain which is still available to the connoisseur. Porcelain pieces of the 18th century, primarily are depicted; however, as a matter of comparison and completeness, later production of some of the existing old factories and a few examples of several modern establishments are presented for the observation of the amateur as well as the connoisseur. The pictures are arranged by consecutive numbers in practically the same chronological sequence as the factories are discussed in Chapters III and IV. The brief title under each illustration indicates the name or type of the item, manufacturer, approximate date of production, possessor, and in many instances the modeler or decorator. In addition, such special features as styles, color, method of decoration and other pertinent information are given. In all cases a cross-reference number in parentheses refers to the page of the text where more information on the piece is found.

Fig. 1 Böttger's Red Stoneware Vase. About 1710—15
(Pages 16, 20 and 42).
The Cleveland Museum of Art, Cleveland

MEISSEN

Fig. 2 Böttger's Stoneware Tea-pots, Polished and Lacquered. About 1715 (Pages 16, 20 and 42).
Museum für Kunst und Gewerbe, Hamburg

Fig. 3 Böttger's Porcelain Vase. Before 1720 (Pages 16, 20 and 42).
The Metropolitan Museum of Art, New York

Fig. 4 Böttger's Porcelain Chinese Incense Figure. About 1718—20
(Pages 16, 20 and 42). *Collection of George W. Ware*

MEISSEN

Fig. 5 Bowl with Chinoiseries in Gold Silhouette,
Probably Painted by an Augsburg Hausmaler. About 1720 (Pages 20 and 44).
The Metropolitan Museum of Art, New York

Fig. 6 Pot and Sugar Bowls with Chinoiseries in Gold. About 1722 (Pages 20 and 44).
Bayerisches Nationalmuseum, Munich

MEISSEN

Fig. 7 Cup and Saucer Decorated with Polychrome Chinoiseries. About 1725—30
(Pages 20 and 44). *Collection of George W. Ware*

Fig. 8 Pots with Polychrome Chinoiseries after J. G. Höroldt. About 1725—30
(Pages 20 and 44). *In Private Possession, Berlin*

MEISSEN

Fig. 9 Octagon Plate with Rich Gold Lace Decorations and Pictures.
About 1740 (Page 44). *Museum für Kunst und Gewerbe, Hamburg*

Fig. 10 Cup and Saucer and Tea-pot with Amusing Decorations of Fable Animals,
by F. A. von Löwenfink. About 1735 (Page 44). *Collection of Mrs. Charles B. Stout, Memphis*

MEISSEN

Fig. 11 Vase with Lid and Swan Handles, by J. J. Kändler. About 1735—38
(Page 46). *City Art Museum, Saint Louis*

MEISSEN

Fig. 12 Plate from the "Yellow Tiger Service." About 1728 (Page 47).
Collection of Karl Mossner, Berlin

Fig. 13 Large Plate from the "Red Dragon Service." About 1730 (Page 47).
Collection of Karl Mossner, Berlin

Fig. 14 Plate with Saxon-Polish Coat of Arms, 1733 (Page 47).
Collection of Karl Mossner, Berlin

Fig. 15 Large Plate from the Service of Count Sulkowski, 1735—37 (Page 47).
Schlossmuseum, Berlin

MEISSEN

Fig. 16 Tureen from the Service of Count Sulkowski, by J. J. Kändler, in Baroque Style, 1735—36 (Pages 21 and 47). *Schlossmuseum, Berlin*

MEISSEN

Fig. 17 Siren with Candydish from the "Swan Service" of Count Brühl,
by J. J. Kändler and J. F. Eberlein, 1737—41 (Page 47). *Schlossmuseum, Berlin*

MEISSEN

Fig. 18 Tureen from the "Swan Service" of Count Brühl, in Baroque Style,
by J. J. Kändler, 1737—41 (Pages 21 and 47). *Schlossmuseum, Berlin*

MEISSEN

Fig. 19 Two Golden Orioles, by J. J. Kändler. About 1734 (Page 47).
Schlossmuseum, Berlin

Fig. 20 A Buck, by J. J. Kändler. About 1732 (Page 47).
Schlossmuseum, Berlin

MEISSEN

Fig. 21 Harlequin Sitting on Stump, by J. J. Kändler. About 1738 (Page 47).
Collection of Irwin Untermyer, New York
Photograph, Courtesy of Metropolitan Museum of Art, New York

MEISSEN

Fig. 22 Pair Playing Mandolin, by J. J. Kändler. About 1740 (Page 47).
Staatliche Porzellansammlung, Dresden

Fig. 23 Kissing Couple, by J. J. Kändler. About 1740 (Page 47).
Wadsworth Atheneum, Hartford

MEISSEN

Fig. 24 Crinoline Group, "Beltrame and Colombina", by J. J. Kändler. About 1740
(Page 47). *Schlossmuseum, Berlin*

Fig. 25 Cavalier and Lady in Crinoline, by J. J. Kändler. About 1744 (Page 47).
Formerly Darmstädter Collection, Berlin

MEISSEN

Fig. 26 Lady in Laced Cap and Flowered Crinoline, by J. J. Kändler. About 1744 (Page 47).
Collection of Irwin Untermyer, New York
Photograph, Courtesy of Metropolitan Museum of Art, New York

MEISSEN

Fig. 27 Monk and Nun, by J. J. Kändler. About 1740 (Page 47).
Bayerisches Nationalmuseum, Munich

MEISSEN

Fig. 28 "The Goose Deal" on Bronze Base, by J. J. Kändler. About 1745 (Page 47).
(Formerly, Collection of Hermine Feist) Schlossmuseum, Berlin

MEISSEN

Fig. 29 Turk with Spanish Horse, by J. J. Kändler. About 1748 (Page 47).
Wadsworth Atheneum, Hartford

MEISSEN

Fig. 30 Dessert Plate with "Brühl" Mixture of Flowers and Fruits, 1742
(Page 47). *Collection of George W. Ware*

Fig. 31 Covered Soup-cup with Shadow-flowers, in Baroque Style.
About 1738 (Pages 21 and 47). *In Private Possession, Berlin*

MEISSEN

Fig. 32 Chocolate-pot with East-Asiatic Relief Decorations. Probably about 1740 (Page 44)
Collection of Katherine Holtzclaw, Atlanta

Fig. 33 Water-pitcher with Siren Handle. About 1750—55 (Pages 44 and 48).
Collection of George W. Ware

Fig. 34 Tankard with Flower Paintings and Silver Top with Medallion of August the Strong.
About 1745 (Pages 44 and 48). *Collection of Ross T. Silkett, Washington*

MEISSEN

Fig. 35 Covered Vase with Gilded Bronze Mounting, in Rococo Style.
About 1760 (Pages 21 and 48). *(Formerly Collection of J. P. Morgan).*
The Cleveland Museum of Art, Cleveland

MEISSEN

Fig. 36 Porcelain Temple, in Rococo Style, by J. J. Kändler. About 1750 (Pages 21 and 48).
Schlossmuseum, Berlin

MEISSEN

Fig 37 Count Rohan and Marchioness Pompadour as "Acis and Galathee", by J. J. Kändler,
According to a Picture by C. N. Cochin. About 1755 (Pages 21 and 48). *Schlossmuseum, Berlin*

Fig. 38 "The Judgment of Paris", by J. J. Kändler. About 1772 (Page 49).
Wadsworth Atheneum, Hartford

MEISSEN

Fig. 39 Theater Group "Annette and Lubin", after M. V. Acier. About 1780 (Page 49).
Museum für Kunst und Gewerbe, Hamburg

MEISSEN

Fig. 40 Cup and Saucer with Rural Scenes after D. Teniers, and Basket Weave Osier Rim.
About 1755—60 (Pages 36 and 48). *Collection of G. Ryland Scott, Memphis*

Fig. 41 Tureen Decorated with Flowers and Osier Rim, in Rococo Style.
About 1760 (Pages 21, 36, 44 and 48). *In Private Possession, Berlin*

MEISSEN

Fig. 42 Dish of the Saxon Court with Colored Flowers and Green Watteau Scenes.
About 1765 (Page 48). *Collection of E. W. Braun, Nürnberg*

Fig. 43 Tray Painted and Trimmed in Louis Seize Style, by J. G. Loehnig.
About 1780 (Pages 22 and 49). *The Art Institute of Chicago, Chicago*

MEISSEN

Fig. 44 Parts of a Breakfast Service with Colored Hunting Scenes. About 1770 (Page 49).
In Private Possession, Berlin

Fig. 45 Parts of a Coffee Service with Blue and Gold Flowers and Gold Rim.
About 1775 (Pages 44 and 49). *M. H. de Young Memorial Museum, San Francisco*

MEISSEN

Fig. 46 Parts of a Coffee Service with Early Maroon Background.
About 1850—60 (Page 50). *Collection of George W. Ware*

MEISSEN

Fig. 47 Figure Nut Bowls, from an Old Model by J. J. Kändler.
Last Part of the 19th Century (Page 50).   *Collection of George W. Ware*

Fig. 48 White Fish Otter, by M. Esser, 1926 (Pages 24 and 50).
Fig. 49 Spaniard with Lute, by P. Scheurich, 1934 (Pages 24 and 50).
Staatliche Porzellan-Manufaktur, Meissen

MEISSEN

Fig. 50 Lady with Moor, by P. Scheurich, 1919 (Page 50).
Staatliche Porzellan-Manufaktur, Meissen

MEISSEN

Fig. 51 Tureen with Cover. About 1725—30 (Pages 51 and 52).
The Art Institute of Chicago, Chicago

Fig. 52 Bowl with Black Decoration and Gilding, in Baroque Style.
About 1730 (Pages 21 and 51). *Museo Civico, Turin*

VIENNA, DU PAQUIER'S FACTORY

Fig. 53 Large Plate with East-Asiatic Decoration. About 1730 (Page 51).
Germanisches Nationalmuseum, Nürnberg

Fig. 54 Cup and Saucer Decorated with East-Asiatic Scenes. About 1730—35 (Page 51).
The Art Institute of Chicago, Chicago

VIENNA, DU PAQUIER'S FACTORY

Fig. 55 Hood Maker with Model. About 1760 (Page 52).
Bayerisches Nationalmuseum, Munich

Fig. 56 White Harlequin. About 1750 (Page 52).
Bayerisches Nationalmuseum, Munich

Fig. 57 Unpainted White Group, by J. J. Niedermeyer. About 1755 (Page 52).
Oesterreichisches Museum für Angewandte Kunst, Vienna

VIENNA

Fig. 58 Shepherd and Shepherdess. About 1765 (Pages 52 and 53).
Collection of George W. Ware

VIENNA

Fig. 59 "Declaration of Love". About 1770 (Pages 52 and 53).
Bayerisches Nationalmuseum, Munich

VIENNA

Fig. 60 Plate with Colored Exhibition of the Death of Mark Antony.
Dated 1805 (Page 53). *Germanisches Nationalmuseum, Nürnberg*

Fig. 61 Cup and Saucer with High-Gold Frieze Decoration, in Empire Style.
Dated 1799 (Pages 23 and 53).
Germanisches Nationalmuseum, Nürnberg

VIENNA

Fig. 62 Cup and Saucer Decorated with Oval Medallions on Imitation Mosaic Background.
Dated 1800 (Page 53). *Philadelphia Museum of Art, Philadelphia*

Fig. 63 Cup and Saucer with Cupid Painting and Gold Border. Dated 1800 (Page 53).
Philadelphia Museum of Art, Philadelphia

VIENNA

Fig. 64 Cup and Saucer Decorated with Various Materials and Gold Border.
Dated 1799 (Page 53). *Philadelphia Museum of Art, Philadelphia*

Fig. 65 Chocolate Service Completely Gilded, Picture of Brandenburg Gate on Tray.
About 1830 (Pages 23 and 53). *Philadelphia Museum of Art, Philadelphia*

VIENNA

Fig. 66 Coffee-pot Painted in Purple, Red and Gold, by J. Aufenwerth. About 1720 (Page 55).
Schlossmuseum, Berlin

HAUSMALEREI, AUGSBURG

Fig. 67 Tea-pot Decorated in Red and Black in the Preissler Workshop, Kronstadt.
Painting about 1725–35 (Page 55). *Victoria and Albert Museum, London*

Fig. 68 Tea Service with Purple Decoration, by I. Bottengruber, Breslau.
About 1730 (Page 55). *Schlossmuseum, Berlin*

HAUSMALEREI, KRONSTADT AND BRESLAU

Fig. 69 Dish with Diamond-point Engraving, by A. O. E. von dem Busch, Hildesheim. Dated and Signed 1754 (Page 56). *Victoria and Albert Museum, London*

Fig. 70 Plate with Dancer and Musician, Painted by F. F. Mayer, Pressnitz. About 1760 (Page 56). *Schlossmuseum, Berlin*

HAUSMALEREI, HILDESHEIM AND PRESSNITZ

Fig. 71 Ladies in Conversation. About 1755—60 (Pages 21 and 58).
Musées Royaux d'Art et d'Histoire, Brussels

HÖCHST

Fig. 72 The Arts and Sciences Honor the Chinese Emperor. About 1760 (Page 58).
Museum für Kunst und Gewerbe, Hamburg

HÖCHST

Fig. 73 Chinese Empress with Attendant, Probably by L. Russinger. About 1760 (Page 58).
Schlossmuseum, Berlin

HÖCHST

Fig. 74 "Calvary", by J. P. Melchior. About 1770 (Page 59).
Schlossmuseum, Berlin

HÖCHST

Figs. 75 and 76 "The Frightened Children", by J. P. Melchior. About 1770–75 (Page 59).
Museum für Kunsthandwerk, Frankfurt on Main

Fig. 77 Boy and Girl Resting, by J. P. Melchior. About 1770 (Page 59).
Musées Royaux d'Art et d'Histoire, Brussels

HÖCHST

Fig. 78 "The Grape Thief". About 1775—80 (Page 59).
Museum für Kunsthandwerk, Frankfurt on Main

HÖCHST

Fig. 79 "Venus and Amor", by J. P Melchior. About 1775 (Pages 23 and 59).
Museum für Kunsthandwerk, Frankfurt on Main

HÖCHST

Fig. 80 Dish with Lilac Paintings and Gilded Borders. About 1760 (Page 59).
Victoria and Albert Museum, London

Fig. 81 "Potpourri" Vases, in Rococo Fashion. About 1765—70 (Pages 21 and 59).
Museum für Kunsthandwerk, Frankfurt on Main

HÖCHST

Fig. 82 Cup and Saucer with Green and Brown Landscape. About 1770 (Page 59).
Collection of J. Kenneth Krug, New York
Fig. 83 Blue Bird Candy-box. About 1780 (Page 59).
Collection of George W. Ware

Fig. 84 Triple Connected Vase, "Drillingsbecher". About 1770 (Page 59).
Collection of George W. Ware

HÖCHST

Fig. 85 "Julia" from the Italian Comedy, by F. A. Bustelli. About 1756 (Page 62).
Bayerisches Nationalmuseum, Munich

NYMPHENBURG

Fig. 86 "Pantalone" from the Italian Comedy, by F. A. Bustelli. About 1756 (Page 62).
Bayerisches Nationalmuseum, Munich

NYMPHENBURG

Fig. 87 "Mater Dolorosa" from a Calvary Group, by F. A. Bustelli.
About 1755 (Pages 21 and 62). *Schlossmuseum, Berlin*

NYMPHENBURG

Fig. 88 Lady in Crinoline, by F. A. Bustelli. About 1755 (Page 62).
Bayerisches Nationalmuseum, Munich

Figs. 89 and 90 Figures from the Italian Comedy, by F. A. Bustelli. About 1757 (Page 62).
Bayerisches Nationalmuseum, Munich

NYMPHENBURG

Fig. 91 Bust of Count Sigismund von Haimhausen, by F. A. Bustelli, 1761 (Page 62).
Bayerisches Nationalmuseum, Munich

NYMPHENBURG

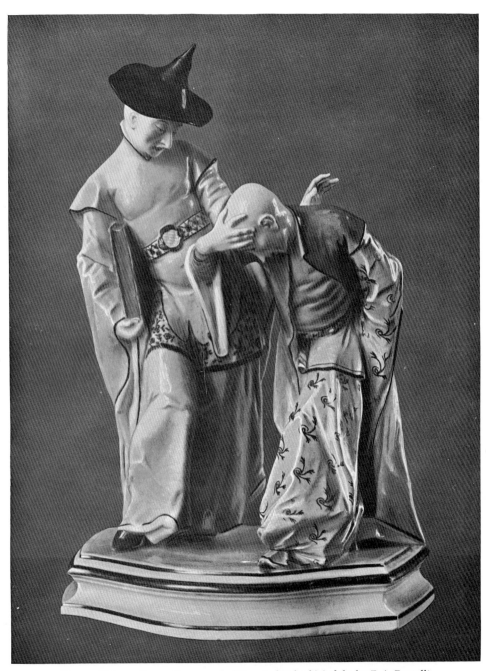

Fig. 92 Chinese Group Composed of Two Individual Models, by F. A. Bustelli.
About 1760 (Page 62). *Bayerisches Nationalmuseum, Munich*

NYMPHENBURG

Fig. 93 "Donna Martina", by F. A. Bustelli. About 1760 (Page 62).
In Private Possession, Munich

NYMPHENBURG

Fig. 94 "Diana" Showing Classical Trend in Porcelain. by J. Kirchmayer.
About 1800 (Pages 23 and 64). *Bayerisches Nationalmuseum, Munich*

Fig. 95 Bear-baiting, by D. Auliczek. After 1765 (Page 62).
Schlossmuseum, Berlin

NYMPHENBURG

Fig. 96 Parts of a Tea Service. About 1755 (Pages 21 and 64).
Bayerisches Nationalmuseum, Munich

Fig. 97 Coffee-pots. About 1760 (Page 64).
Schlossmuseum, Berlin

NYMPHENBURG

Fig. 98 Food Warmer. About 1760—70 (Page 64).
The Art Institute of Chicago, Chicago

Fig. 99 Coffee Service, in Biedermeier Style. About 1810 (Pages 24 and 64)
Bayerisches Nationalmuseum, Munich

NYMPHENBURG

Fig. 100 Bust of King Max I of Bavaria, in Biscuit Porcelain,
by J. P. Melchior. About 1810 (Pages 37 and 64).
Bayerisches Nationalmuseum, Munich

Fig. 101 Portrait Busts of the Two Daughters of King Max I, in Biscuit Porcelain,
by J. P. Melchior. About 1819 (Pages 37 and 64).
Bayerisches Nationalmuseum, Munich

NYMPHENBURG

Fig. 102 Horse Tamer, by J. Wackerle. Modeled in 1941 (Page 64).
Staatliche Porzellan-Manufaktur, Nymphenburg

NYMPHENBURG

Fig. 103 Dancing Pair, by A. K. Luplau. About 1770 (Page 65).
Museum für Kunst und Gewerbe, Hamburg

FÜRSTENBERG

Fig. 104 Coffee-pot with Rocailles and Birds, in Rococo Style. About 1760—65
(Pages 21 and 66). *Museum für Kunst und Gewerbe, Hamburg*

FÜRSTENBERG

Fig. 105 Vase with Cover and Colored Watteau Painting. About 1770 (Page 66).
In Private Possession, Berlin

FÜRSTENBERG

Fig. 106 Tray with Fowl Paintings, Probably by C. G. Albert. About 1770 (Page 66).
Victoria and Albert Museum, London

Fig. 107 Vases in Neo-Classical Style. About 1785—90 (Pages 23 and 66).
Nationalmuseum, Stockholm

FÜRSTENBERG

Fig. 108 Girl with Bird Cage. Between 1751—57 (Page 67).
Schlossmuseum, Berlin

BERLIN, WEGELY'S FACTORY

Fig. 109 Chinese Pair, by F. E. Meyer, 1768 (Page 69).
Schlossmuseum, Berlin

Fig. 110 Cavalier and Lady, by W. C. Meyer, 1769 (Page 69).
Schlossmuseum, Berlin

BERLIN

Fig. 111 "Mars and the History", Allegorical Group in Biscuit.
Neo-Classical Style. By Wilhelm Christian Meyer.
About 1766 (Pages 37 and 69).
Museum für Kunst und Gewerbe, Hamburg

Fig. 112 Clock with the Figure "Future" Perched on Top,
by Friedrich Elias Meyer. About 1770 (Page 69).
*Formerly Owned by the Swedish Queen Luise Ulrike,
Sister of the Prussian King, Frederick the Great
Nationalmuseum, Stockholm*

BERLIN

Figs. 113 and 114 Shapely Figure Draped in Robe, Front and Rear Views.
About 1780—85 (Page 69). *Collection of George W. Ware*

Fig. 115 Gay Shepherds and Shepherdesses. About 1785 (Page 69).
Collection of George W. Ware

BERLIN

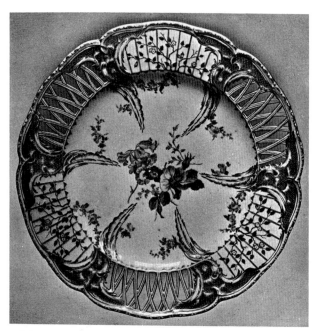

Fig. 116 Dessert Plate from the Service "New Palace of Potsdam", for Frederick the Great, in Rococo Style, 1765—67 (Pages 21 and 69). *Staatliche Porzellan-Manufaktur, Berlin*

Fig. 117 Various Ornamental Plates. Top: Berlin, about 1790; Fürstenberg, about 1770. Bottom: Höchst, 1770; Meissen, about 1755; and Ludwigsburg, about 1770 (Page 69). *Collection of George W. Ware*

BERLIN

Fig. 118 Oval Relief, "Grieninger Receives a Message from the King",
1765 (Page 69). *Museum für Kunst und Gewerbe, Hamburg*

Fig. 119 Dishes and Fruit Center-piece, by F. E. Meyer. About 1770 (Page 69).
Schlossmuseum, Berlin

BERLIN

Fig. 120 Beautifully Decorated Tête-à-Tête. About 1770 (Page 69).
(From the Collection of Thiers)
Musée du Louvre, Paris

Fig. 121 Solitaire "Minna von Barnhelm", after Etchings by D. Chodowiecki.
About 1771 (Page 69).
Museum für Kunst und Gewerbe, Hamburg

BERLIN

Fig. 122 Cup and Saucer "Winter" Colored with Gold Paintings, in Biedermeier Style.
After 1800 (Pages 24 and 69). *Staatliche Porzellan-Manufaktur, Berlin*

Fig. 123 Head of Mars from Clock "Mars and Venus", by P. Scheurich, 1940
(Page 70). *Staatliche Porzellan-Manufaktur, Berlin*

BERLIN

Fig. 124 "Toilet of Venus", by W. Lanz. About 1755—60 (Page 71).
Schlossmuseum, Berlin

FRANKENTHAL

Fig. 125 Cavalier with Hat and Lady with Bird Cage, by J. F. Lück. About 1760 (Page 71).
Schlossmuseum, Berlin

Fig. 126 "Harmony" and "Disharmony", by K. G. Lück. About 1765—70 (Page 71).
Schlossmuseum, Berlin

FRANKENTHAL

Fig. 127 "Okeanos", by K. Link. About 1765 (Page 71).
Museum für Kunst und Gewerbe, Hamburg

FRANKENTHAL

Fig. 128 "Thetis", by K. Link. About 1765 (Page 71).
Museum für Kunst und Gewerbe, Hamburg

FRANKENTHAL

Fig. 129 Dancer Adorned with Flowers, by K. G. Lück. About 1765
(Page 71). *Hetjens-Museum, Düsseldorf*

Fig. 130 "Spring, Summer and Autumn", by K. Link. About 1765 (Page 71).
Schlossmuseum, Berlin

FRANKENTHAL

Fig. 131 "Meleager and Atalante", by K. Link, 1777 (Page 71).
Museum für Kunst und Gewerbe, Hamburg

FRANKENTHAL

Fig. 132 Tea-pot with Hunting Scenes, in Rococo Style. About 1755—59 (Pages 21 and 72).
Schlossmuseum, Berlin

Fig. 133 Chessmen. About 1765 (Page 72). *Schlossmuseum, Berlin*

FRANKENTHAL

Fig. 134 Dish Painted after J. E. Nilson's Etching "Peace Time Gladness".
About 1765 (Page 72). *Museum für Kunst und Gewerbe, Hamburg*

Fig. 135 Large Plate Decorated with Birds, in Sèvres Style. About 1771
(Pages 22 and 72). *Bayerisches Nationalmuseum, Munich*

FRANKENTHAL

Fig. 136 Dancing Pair as Gardeners. About 1760 (Page 75).
Schlossmuseum, Berlin

LUDWIGSBURG

Fig. 137 Female Fisher, by J. C. W. Beyer. About 1760—65 (Page 75).
Schlossmuseum, Berlin

LUDWIGSBURG

Figs. 138 and 139 Singer and Drinker, by J. C. W. Beyer. About 1765 (Page 75).
Schlossmuseum, Berlin

Fig. 140 Spinet and Cello Players, by J. C. W. Beyer. About 1760—65 (Page 75).
Schlossmuseum, Berlin

LUDWIGSBURG

Fig. 141 Candlestick with Child Figures and Flowers and with the Coat of Arms
of Giovanelli-Martinengo, by G. F. Riedel. About 1762 (Page 75).
Württembergisches Landesmuseum, Stuttgart

Fig. 142 Roman Goddess or Muse, with no Definite Attribute
to Specify any Particular Mythological Figure,
in Neo-Classical Style. About 1775 (Pages 23 and 76).
Collection of George W. Ware

LUDWIGSBURG

Fig. 143 Tea-pot with Coat of Arms of Giovanelli-Martinengo, by G. F. Riedel. About 1762 (Page 76). *Württembergisches Landesmuseum, Stuttgart*

Fig. 144 "Potpourri" Vase with Ladies and Gentlemen in Landscape. About 1765 (Pages 21 and 76). *Museum für Kunst und Gewerbe, Hamburg*

LUDWIGSBURG

Fig. 145 Plate with Landscape Paintings and Osier Relief Border.
About 1770 (Page 76). *Collection of George W. Ware*

Fig. 146 Plate with "Venus and Amor", in Neo-Classical Style.
About 1775 (Pages 23 and 76).
Museum für Kunst und Gewerbe, Hamburg

LUDWIGSBURG

Fig. 147 Coffee-pot Painted in Crimson Monochrome and Gold. About 1760 (Page 78).
Victoria and Albert Museum, London

ANSBACH

Fig. 148 Lady and Gentleman under Trellis. About 1765 (Page 78).
Bayerisches Nationalmuseum, Munich

ANSBACH

Fig. 149 Court Figure, Probably Ansbach. About 1770 (Page 78).
Bernisches Historisches Museum, Bern

Fig. 150 Cup with Initials. About 1770 (Page 78).
Collection of Adolf Bayer, Ansbach

ANSBACH

Fig. 151 Soldiers Agreeing upon a Truce, by K. Vogelmann. About 1761—65 (P
Collection of R. Thornton Wilson
Photograph, Courtesy of Metropolitan Museum, New York

KELSTERBACH

Fig. 152 Lady and Gentleman. About 1765 (Page 81).
Germanisches Nationalmuseum, Nürnberg

Fig. 153 Two Masked Figures from the Italian Comedy, Probably by L. Russinger.
About 1770 (Page 81). *Museum für Kunst und Gewerbe, Hamburg*

FULDA

Fig. 154 Group of Musicians under Trellis. About 1770—75 (Page 81).
Schlossmuseum, Berlin

FULDA

Fig. 155 Lady and Cavalier. About 1775 (Page 81).
Schlossmuseum, Berlin

FULDA

Fig. 156 Tobacco Box with Gallant Figures. About 1765 (Page 81).
Schlossmuseum, Berlin

Fig. 157 Food Warmer with Neo-Classical Decorations. About 1770
(Page 81). *Staatliche Kunstsammlungen, Kassel*

FULDA

Fig. 158 Coffee-pot Painted in Colors. About 1770 (Page 80).
Victoria and Albert Museum, London

Fig. 159 Porcelain Case with Purple Painting. About 1765 (Page 80).
Museum für Kunst und Gewerbe, Hamburg

Fig. 160 Tureen, Painted by F. K. Wohlfahrt. About 1770 (Page 80).
Museum für Kunst und Gewerbe, Hamburg

OTTWEILER (NASSAU-SAARBRÜCKEN)

Fig. 161 Horse Tamer, by J. G. Pahland, after a Sandstone Model by J. A. Nahl.
About 1770 (Page 82).
Museum für Kunst und Gewerbe, Hamburg

KASSEL

Fig. 162 Coffee-pot Decorated with Harbor Scenes. About 1765 (Page 82).
Victoria and Albert Museum, London

GUTENBRUNN (PFALZ-ZWEIBRÜCKEN)

Fig. 163 Large Vase with a Variety of Decorations. About 1770 (Page 85).
Victoria and Albert Museum, London

VOLKSTEDT-RUDOLSTADT

Fig. 164 Cello Player. Wallendorf. About 1770—80 (Page 86).
Bayerisches Nationalmuseum, Munich

Fig. 165 Girl on Lounge. Kloster Veilsdorf. About 1770 (Page 85).
Bayerisches Nationalmuseum, Munich

WALLENDORF AND KLOSTER VEILSDORF

Fig. 166 Decked Cups and Saucers with Neo-Classical Brown Monochrome Decorations. Gera.
About 1780 (Page 87). *Collection of George W. Ware*

Fig. 167 Cup and Saucer with River Scenes in Monochrome. Ilmenau.
Late 18th Century (Page 87). *The Metropolitan Museum of Art, New York*

GERA AND ILMENAU

Fig. 168 Tête-à-Tête. Gotha. About 1780 (Pages 23 and 84).
Museum für Kunst und Gewerbe, Hamburg

Fig. 169 Lady and Cavalier Representing "Summer". Limbach. About 1775 (Page 87).
Germanisches Nationalmuseum, Nürnberg

GOTHA AND LIMBACH

Fig. 170 Lady and Cavalier with Flowers. Sitzendorf. Late 19th Century
(Page 89). *Collection of George W. Ware*

Fig. 171 Boy and Girl with Fruits and Flowers. Volkstedt-Rudolstadt.
Modern (Page 86). *Collection of George W. Ware*

SITZENDORF AND VOLKSTEDT-RUDOLSTADT

Fig. 172 "Emperor's Waltz", by L. Friedrich-Gronau. Modern (Page 89).
Rosenthal-Porzellan AG, Selb

ROSENTHAL

Fig. 173 A Spirited Steed, by P. Scheurich. Modern (Page 89).
Porzellanfabrik Lorenz Hutschenreuther, Selb

HUTSCHENREUTHER·

Fig. 174 Graceful Modeling in Useful Wares. Modern (Page 89).
Heinrich and Co., Selb

HEINRICH

MUSEUMS CONTRIBUTING REPRODUCTIONS

AMERICAN MUSEUMS

City Art Museum, Saint Louis, Missouri

M. H. De Young Memorial Museum, San Francisco, California

Philadelphia Museum of Art, Philadelphia, Pennsylvania

The Art Institute of Chicago, Chicago, Illinois

The Cleveland Museum of Art, Cleveland, Ohio

The Metropolitan Museum of Art, New York, New York

Wadsworth Atheneum, Hartford, Connecticut

EUROPEAN MUSEUMS

Bayerisches Nationalmuseum, Munich, Germany

Bernisches Historisches Museum, Bern, Switzerland

Germanisches Nationalmuseum, Nürnberg, Germany

Hetjens-Museum, Düsseldorf, Germany

Musée du Louvre, Paris, France

Musées Royaux D'Art et D'Histoire, Brussels, Belgium

Museo Civico, Turin, Italy

Museum für Kunst und Gewerbe, Hamburg, Germany

Museum für Kunsthandwerk, Frankfurt on Main, Germany

Nationalmuseum, Stockholm, Sweden

Österreichisches Museum für angewandte Kunst, Vienna, Austria

Schlossmuseum, Berlin, Germany

Staatliche Kunstsammlungen, Kassel, Germany

Staatliche Porzellansammlung, Dresden, Germany

Victoria and Albert Museum, London, England

Württembergisches Landesmuseum, Stuttgart, Germany

The museums and the several factories and individual collectors who provided photographs are given credit beneath their respective contributions.

AUCTION AND COLLECTION CATALOGS

Sammlung Emma Budge, Hamburg
Auction Catalog Paul Graupe, Berlin 1937

Sammlung Fritz Clemm
Auction Catalog Rudolf Lepke, No. 1497, Berlin 1907

Sammlung Darmstädter, Berlin
Europäisches Porzellan des 18. Jahrhunderts.   Revised by L. Schnorr von Carolsfeld
Auction Catalog Rudolf Lepke, No. 1933, Berlin 1925

Sammlung Hermann Embden, Hamburg
Auction Catalog Rudolf Lepke, No. 1524, Berlin 1908

Sammlung C. H. Fischer, Dresden.   Revised by Otto von Falke
Auction Catalog Hugo Helbing, Munich 1918

Sammlung Gustav von Gerhardt, Budapest.   Meissner Porzellan
Auction Catalog Rudolf Lepke, No. 1623, Berlin 1911

Sammlung Erich von Goldschmidt-Rothschild
Auction Catalog Hermann Ball and Paul Graupe, Berlin 1931

Sammlung Georg Hirth, München, 2 Volumes
G. Hirth, Publishing House, Munich 1916

Sammlung Carl Jourdan, Frankfurt am Main
Auction Catalog Rudolf Lepke, No. 1585, Berlin 1910

Porzellansammlung von Klemperer
Revised by L. Schnorr von Carolsfeld, Dresden 1928

Wiener-Porzellan-Sammlung Karl Mayer
Auction Catalog Auktionshaus für Altertümer, Glückselig-GmbH., Vienna 1928

Sammlung Margarete Oppenheim
Auction Catalog Julius Böhler, Munich 1936

Sammlung Margarete und Franz Oppenheimer.   Meissner Porzellan, 3 Volumes
Revised by L. Schnorr von Carolsfeld, Dresden 1928

Sammlungen Rüttgers, München, und Sönksen, London-Plön
Auction Catalog Hugo Helbing, Munich 1927

Sammlung Jean Wurz, Mannheim.   Frankenthaler Porzellan
Auction Catalog Rudolf Lepke, No. 1927, Berlin 1924

The above list of auction and collection catalogs is arranged alphabetically in the original spelling. These catalogs which are fully illustrated contain complete descriptions of all items and are excellent references as explained on page 26.

BIBLIOGRAPHY

BOOKS IN ENGLISH

Avery, C. Louise	Masterpieces of European Porcelain *The Metropolitan Museum of Art, New York, 1949*
Cox, Warren E.	Pottery and Porcelain, *Crown Publishers, New York, 1945*
Ducret, Siegfried	Unknown Porcelain of the 18th Century, *(Translated by John Hayward)* *Frankfurt am Main, 1956*
Eberlein, H. D. and Ramsdell, R. W.	The Practical Book of Chinaware, *Lippincott Company, New York, 1948*
Hannover, E.	Pottery and Porcelain, *(Edited by Bernard Rackham), London, 1925*
Honey, W. B.	Dresden China, *Faber & Faber, London, 1946*
Honey, W. B.	German Porcelain, *Faber & Faber, London, 1947*
Honey, W. B.	History of Ceramic Art, *Faber & Faber, London, 1949*
Lichfield, Frederick	Pottery and Porcelain, *London, 1912*
McClellan, George B.	The McClellan Collection of German and Austrian Porcelain *Privately Printed, New York, 1946*
Penkala, Maria	European Porcelain, *A. Zwemmer, London, 1947*
Pickman, D. L.	The Golden Age of European Porcelain, *Boston, 1939*
Rosenfeld, David	Porcelain Figures of the Eighteenth Century *Studio Publications, New York, 1949*
Schmidt, Robert	Porcelain as an Art and a Mirror of Fashion *(Translated by W. A. Thorpe), London, 1932*
Thorn, C. Jordan	Handbook of Old Pottery and Porcelain Marks *Tudor Publishing Co, New York, 1947*

BOOKS IN GERMAN

Albiker, Carl	Die Meissner Porzellantiere im 18. Jahrhundert, *Berlin, 1935*
Balet, L.	Ludwigsburger Porzellan, *Stuttgart and Leipzig, 1911*
Bauer-Paulfranz, L.	Fabrikmarken-ABC, *Coburg, 1930*
Bayer, Adolf	Ansbacher Porzellan, *Ansbach, 1933*
Berling, K.	Festschrift zur 200jährigen Jubelfeier der ältesten europäischen Porzellanmanufaktur Meissen, *Dresden, 1911*
Brüning, Adolf	Porzellan, *Berlin, 1914*
Christ, Hans	Ludwigsburger Porzellanfiguren, *Stuttgart, 1921*
Doenges, Willy	Meissner Porzellan. Seine Geschichte und künstlerische Entwicklung *Dresden, 1921*

227

Ducret, Siegfried	Unbekannte Porzellane des 18. Jahrhunderts, *Frankfurt am Main, 1956*
Ernst, Richard	Wiener Porzellan des Klassizismus, *Vienna, 1925*
Falke, Otto von	Deutsche Porzellanfiguren, *Berlin, 1919*
Folnesics, J. and Braun, E. W.	Geschichte der K. K. Wiener Porzellanmanufaktur, *Vienna, 1907*
Graesse, J. G. Th. and Jaennicke, E.	Führer für Sammler von Porzellan, Fayence etc., *Berlin, 1921*
Heuser, E.	Pfälzisches Porzellan des 18. Jahrhunderts, *Speyer, 1907*
Heuser, E.	Porzellan von Strassburg und Frankenthal, *Neustadt a. d. Hardt, 1922*
Hofmann, F. H.	Frankenthaler Porzellan, *Munich, 1911*
Hofmann, F. H.	Geschichte der bayerischen Porzellan-Manufaktur Nymphenburg *Leipzig, 1922*
Hofmann, F. H.	Das Porzellan der europäischen Manufakturen im 18. Jahrhundert *Berlin, 1932*
Josten, H. H.	Fuldaer Porzellanfiguren, *Berlin, 1929*
Lenz, G.	Berliner Porzellan: Die Manufaktur Friedrichs des Großen, *Berlin, 1913*
Lunghard, Rudolf	Vorlesungen der Meisterschule für Porzellan, Staatliche Fachschule in Selb
Oppenheim, Michel	Johann Peter Melchior als Modellmeister in Höchst *Frankfurt am Main, 1957*
Pazaurek, G. E.	Deutsche Fayence- und Porzellan-Hausmaler, *Leipzig, 1925*
Pazaurek, G. E.	Meissner Porzellanmalerei des 18. Jahrhunderts, *Stuttgart, 1929*
Pelka, O.	Keramik der Neuzeit, *Leipzig, 1924*
Röder, Kurt and Oppenheim, Michel	Das Höchster Porzellan auf der Jahrtausend-Ausstellung in Mainz 1925 *Mainz, 1930*
Röder, Kurt	Das Kelsterbacher Porzellan, *Darmstadt, 1931*
Sauerlandt, Max	Deutsche Porzellan-Figuren des 18. Jahrhunderts, *Cologne, 1923*
Scherer, C.	Das Fürstenberger Porzellan, *Berlin, 1909*
Schmidt, Robert	Das Porzellan als Kunstwerk und Kulturspiegel, *Munich, 1925*
Schnorr von Carolsfeld, L.	Porzellan der europäischen Fabriken des 18. Jahrhunderts, *Berlin, 1920*
Schönberger, Arno	Deutsches Porzellan, *Munich, 1949*
Stieda, W.	Die Porzellanfabrik zu Volkstedt im 18. Jahrhundert, *Leipzig, 1910*
Strohmer-Nowak	Altwiener Porzellan, *Vienna, 1946*
Wanner-Brandt, O.	Album der Erzeugnisse der ehemaligen Württembergischen Manufaktur Alt-Ludwigsburg, *Stuttgart, 1906*
Zimmermann, E.	Die Erfindung und Frühzeit des Meissner Porzellans, *Berlin, 1908*
Zimmermann, E.	Meissner Porzellan, *Leipzig, 1926*

GLOSSARY

Alchemy	The medieval forerunner of the modern science of chemistry. It was chiefly concerned with such problems as turning base metals into gold.
Arcanist	One who possesses the secret of making porcelain.
Arcanum	The latin word for secret or secret remedy.
Baroque Style	The artistic and architectural style which prevailed in progressive periods from about 1600 to 1720 and which appeared in the form and decoration of porcelain from 1710 to about 1740. The Baroque is characterized by its massive form, great contrast of shadows and light, and by vigorous movement.
Biedermeier Style	A German translation and continuation of the Empire style which predominated from about 1820 to 1845. Its forms and decorations typify the comparatively simple tastes of the middleclass people, *bourgeois*, who became prominent at that time. To a certain extent it is identical with the early Victorian.
Biscuit Porcelain	A white marble-like unglazed hard porcelain, usually twice fired, which is used especially in producing figures and other artistic items.
Body	See "Paste."
Bossierer	See "Repairer."
Böttger Porzellan	The first true glazed, smoky-white hard-paste porcelain produced in Europe by Böttger, in Meissen, about 1709.
Böttger Steinzeug	An extremely hard red or dark brown fine-grained stoneware — the higher the firing temperature, the darker the color. It was discovered by Böttger in about 1708 in his attempt to make porcelain.
Cartouches	Ornamental scroll-like designs used for framing paintings of people, landscapes and other subjects on porcelain particularly during the Rococo period.
Ceramics	The art of making articles of baked clay including pottery, porcelain, and all kinds of earthenware.
China	See "Porcelain."
Chinoiseries	Brilliant monochrome, polychrome and gilded paintings depicting the mythological carefree existence of Far Eastern peoples and landscapes, which were employed especially by Höroldt and his associates at MEISSEN beginning about 1721, as well as some of the *Hausmaler* and painters in other factories.

229

Classicism	An expression denoting the influence of the Greeks and Romans. Classicism typifies simplicity, dignity, sobriety and formal proportion.
Comedy	A special kind of performance which prevailed primarily during the 17th and 18th centuries in the court theaters in Italy, Germany and France. These plays, usually of a merry or comedy nature, inspired MEISSEN NYMPHENBURG, HÖCHST and other factories to produce interesting figures of comediennes, comedians and harlequins in great variety.
Crinoline	Long, full, artistically proportioned hoop-skirt used on some female figures particularly by Kändler and other modelers during the late Baroque, Regence and Rococo periods.
Decoration	The application of paints and gilding, or the employment of impressions or reliefs of plastic materials to embellish the appearance of original plain porcelain.
Deutsche Blumen	German or natural flowers which were used for decorating porcelain. The flower paintings were made first from engravings or paintings of flowers and later, after 1740, from natural flowers. They are contrasted with Indian flowers, *Indianische Blumen*, which they succeeded.
Earthenware	A term used to include all glazed and unglazed pottery, especially the coarser kinds, excluding porcelain and stonewares.
Embosser	See "Repairer."
Embossing	The application of plastic ornaments or the joining together of separate pieces of porcelain to complete a whole.
Empire Style	A French Neo-Classical style which predominated from about 1800 to 1820 primarily during the reign of Napoleon (1804–1814). It is characterized by straight lines and symmetry as a result of Egyptian, Greek and Roman influences.
Enamel	A non-transparent colored glaze usually applied over harder glazes and fired at a low temperature. When applied on biscuit it is similar to regular glaze but, as a rule, is not so hard.
Engravings	Decorations or numbers applied on porcelain, either before or after firing, by the use of a pointed instrument or emery wheel.
Faience	A slightly calcareous pottery clay of yellowish or brown color which is opaque and porous and can be scratched with a steel knife. It is distinguished from other types of pottery in that it is coated with a non-transparent, white tin glaze. *Faience* and *Steingut* both are intended to imitate porcelain but are only substitutes. *Faience* is the same material as *Majolica*.
Falsification	Counterfeit or deceptive materials or manipulations employed in copying or changing the form, decoration or mark of a piece of porcelain so it will appear as an original of greater value.

Feldspar	Any of a group of crystal minerals, aluminium silicates with potassium, calcium or barium, and an essential constituent of nearly all crystalline rocks. It is usually white or pinkish and composes about 25 per cent of the ingredients of porcelain.
Firing	A term used for burning or baking porcelain and other ceramic products in producing the finished item.
Flint	A very hard kind of quartz which, when heated, softens, turns white and opaque and can be crushed into a powder and mixed with potter's clay. It can withstand high temperatures.
Flux	Any substance or mixture as silicates, limestone and fluorite used to promote the melting and fusion of metals or minerals. It also causes overglaze colors to vitrify.
Fond Porcelain	The French word *fond* means "ground." Fond porcelains, therefore, are pieces which have a solid monochrome background with reserved white spaces or frames in which paintings of different colors are applied. Fond backgrounds were probably introduced by Höroldt at MEISSEN soon after 1720 and employed as late as 1750 or longer. Typical fond backgrounds were used on many of the "Augustus Rex" (AR) vases. The characteristic fond colors of the early period are yellow, green, apple green, violet, light blue, purple, pink and red and underglaze blue.
Foot Rim	The lowest projecting part of a porcelain item, usually an oval or round rim which contacts the sagger when it is fired, and consequently has little if any glaze.
Frit	Ground glass of various kinds composed of silica and alkaline salts which are used as a basis for certain glazes in imparting density to soft porcelain.
Geschirre	The German word for useful porcelain wares such as dishes, cups and saucers, plates, bowls, pots and such items.
Gilder	One who applies gold decorations.
Gilding	Art or practice of overlaying or painting with gold.
Glaze	The liquid glass-like substance used to cover and seal a piece of porcelain after the first firing and before the second high-temperature firing is made. This vitreous coating of porcelain or pottery is transparent as distinguished from enamel.
Hard-Paste Porcelain	See "Porcelain." The hardest type of porcelain, generally meaning true porcelain or china.
Hausmaler	A German expression for an independent painter or painters of porcelain and other ceramics who obtained white or blue underglaze porcelain from the factories and applied decorations privately, usually for resale.

231

The *Hausmaler* were most active soon after porcelain was discovered at MEISSEN, from about 1715 to 1755. Of the porcelains, they decorated those from MEISSEN and VIENNA principally.

Hausmalerei	Porcelain items decorated by private painters, the *Hausmaler*.
Imari Porcelain	Iron-red, sea-green and luminous blue Japanese porcelain wares named after the harbor town of Imari from which it was exported to Europe. It was characteristically decorated with bamboo and cherry blossoms or hedges of brushwood which grew out of stylized rocks. Imari wares were accurately imitated by MEISSEN.
Impressing	Impressing numbers, symbols or decorative designs by mechanical means on porcelain in its plastic state before the first firing.
Indian Flowers	Far Eastern flowers, *Indianische Blumen*, such as the chrysanthemum, peony, aster and more delicate species which were copied in making porcelain decorations particularly during the early periods. They precede and are of different character from the German flowers, *Deutsche Blumen*.
Jeweled Porcelain	Porcelain produced with various small decorative reliefs which are painted or gilded to imitate pearls or jewels.
Jugendstil	A German term meaning "Youth Style" which is usually known by the French designation, *style nouveau*. A trend in applied art which was introduced by the Belgian Henry van de Velde around 1895 and prevailed until about 1910. It is characterized by many curved lines and planes, and was used in porcelain modeling and decoration especially by COPENHAGEN and MEISSEN.
Kaolin	A clay-like material, principally white in color, composed of varying combinations of silicate of aluminium which are difficult to fuse. It fires white and opaque, withstands high temperatures and is the basic material of porcelain, usually comprising about 50 per cent of the porcelain body or paste. The term kaolin technically applies to all forms of porcelain clay which do not discolor during the firing process.
Laub- und Bandelwerk	Ornamental decoration of leaves and ribbons used in the late Gothic period, and employed in porcelain decoration in the early part of the 18th century.
Louis Seize Style	A style originating in France during the time of Louis XVI, depicting a simpler more formal trend of form and decoration. Its influence appeared in porcelain production around 1760—70, and it is the forerunner of the Neo-Classical style.
Majolica	See "Faience."
Marks	Colored or impressed symbols or trade marks employed by factories to distinguish their porcelain wares from those of other establishments.

Molds	Forms, usually made from gypsum or plaster of Paris, which absorb water freely and which are used for molding intricate parts or whole pieces of porcelain.
Monochrome	Painting in a single color, or different shades of a single color or in gold, frequently employed in painting antique porcelain.
Moons	Plastic variations in the body of very old porcelain resulting from imperfections in the paste, and which appear as more translucent irregular shaped "moons" or "tares" of various sizes and shapes when viewed by transmitted light. These defects are helpful to collectors in determining the antiquity of MEISSEN, VIENNA and to some extent some other old porcelains, including FRANKENTHAL, LUDWIGSBURG and NYMPHENBURG.
Neo-Classical Style	A style characterized by simple, quiet symmetrical or straight lines resulting from the influence of Roman and Greek architecture and sculpture. This style was prominent in porcelain modeling and decoration during the last quarter of the 18th and the beginning of the 19th century.
Osier	A decorative relief pattern of willow or basket-weave design generally impressed on the borders of useful wares to embellish them.
Palette	The set or arrangement of colors employed in the painting of porcelain and other materials.
Paste	The plastic body of porcelain which includes kaolin, quartz and feldspar, and perhaps some minor elements.
Pegmatite	A very coarse-grained rock composed of orthoclase, quartz and mica and sometimes substituted for quartz and feldspar in the production of porcelain.
Polychrome	Painting done in several or many colors, as contrasted to monochrome.
Porcelain	Hard-paste or true porcelain is generally referred to as "china" by English speaking peoples because it originated in the country of China, and is called porcelain by most Continental peoples. It is a hard, white, fine-textured, resonant, acid-resistant, impervious, low-heat-conducting material which is usually translucent. It is the highest grade product in the field of ceramics, and is generally composed of about 50 per cent of slowly fusible or nonfusible kaolin, 25 per cent of quartz and about 25 per cent feldspar which under high temperature form a fusible glass and act as a flux. The relative amounts of the three ingredients vary according to the texture desired — the more kaolin, the harder the porcelain. Its special characteristics are: (1) non-porous even when unglazed, (2) cannot be scratched with a steel knife, (3) is naturally of whitish color from the kaolin but the body may be stained various colors by mineral oxides, (4) is usually glazed after the first firing, (5) is more translucent than pottery or stoneware and less translucent than soft-paste porcelain, and (6) it is usually fired two or more times.

Pottery	Usually refers to all classes of baked clay wares with the exception of stoneware and porcelains. It is slightly calcareous clay which has the following characteristics when fired: (1) is porous, (2) can be scratched with a steel knife, (3) is opaque, (4) is usually reddish-brown, yellow, brown or grey depending upon the composition, and (5) may be baked in the sun.
Quartz	A form of silica occurring in hexagonal crystals or crystalline masses. It is the most common of all solid minerals and composes approximately 25 per cent of the porcelain paste.
Regence Style	An interim style prevailing between the Baroque and Rococo which was employed by MEISSEN and VIENNA primarily from 1725 to 1740. It is characterized by curved lines, scrolls and leaves, and a prevalent light, unrestrained air.
Relief Decorations	Plastic decorations applied on the main body of a porcelain item before firing.
Repairer	One who fits the separately-molded pieces of a porcelain item together and smoothes and seals them with a thin slip paste before firing. Such a person is referred to as a *"Bossierer"* in Germany.
Restoration	The term used for repairing a damaged item by mending or replacing the broken pieces or by restoring the decorations.
Rocaille	A French word which applies to forms and decorations, of Rococo fashion, which are employed in modeling bases and supporting parts of porcelain pieces, and also as painted decorative frames for landscapes and figure paintings.
Rococo Style	The artistic and architectural style of French origin which prevailed from about 1720 to 1770 and which predominated the form and decorations of porcelain from about 1735 to 1775, during the height of its artistic excellence. The Rococo motif is characterized by its light graceful design, its fanciful forms, and succession of C- and S-curves and scrolls.
Saggers	Fire-clay boxes used for protecting pieces of porcelain against flaky ashes and flames and to facilitate proper stacking in the kilns.
Schwarzlot Painting	An old technique of applying black, *schwarz*, decorations at first on glass and later on early VIENNA and other European porcelains. The paintings include landscapes and various scenes, and often imitate engravings.
Slip	Mixture of clay materials with the consistency of thick cream. It is frequently the same material as the paste composing the body but is thinned with water.
Soft-paste Porcelain	A porcelain-like material which, because of its combination, is softer, more transparent, and less resonant than true or hard-paste porcelain. It

is usually composed of about one-half clay and one-half glass and small amounts of fluxes.

Steingut The German expression for a white pottery material fired at a higher temperature than *faience* and covered with a translucent lead glaze. *Steingut* is an English innovation which largely replaced *faience* at the end of the 18th century because it was cheaper. There is no English expression for *Steingut* which is commonly referred to as *faience fine*.

Steinzeug See "Stoneware."

Stoneware A porcelaneous type of ware fired at a high temperature, which differs from porcelain in that it is less purified. Its special characteristics are: (1) nonporous even when not glazed, (2) cannot be scratched readily with a steel knife, (3) its natural color is ash-like but under higher temperatures develops a red-brown, (4) is less resonant than hard-paste porcelain but more so than soft-paste, and (5) it is fired usually without saggers at about 1900° F. Stoneware is called *Steinzeug* in German.

Streublumen Small painted flowers scattered at random over the surface of tablewares, and vases. This mode of decoration is used especially by MEISSEN and is referred to as *Meissener Streublümchen*.

Style Distinctive or characteristic mode of form and decoration which gives character and artistic expression to a subject. The styles of porcelain have been greatly influenced by the prevailing styles of architecture and art; however, they generally appeared later than similar architectural styles, the time-lag varying somewhat among the different factories.

Tares See "Moons."

Terra cotta A pottery material coated with a fine slip or glaze used in the facing of buildings and for relief ornaments, statuettes, urns and other objects.

Thrower A craftsman who forms flat or cylindrical porcelain items such as plates, bowls and vases at the potter's wheel by using his hands or mechanical aids to attain the desired shape and thickness.

Underglaze A term referring to a painting or mark applied under the glaze on once fired porcelain before the glazing and second firing. Because of the high temperature of the second firing, only a few underglaze colors can be used successfully. Cobalt blue is the first and best known, being used many centuries by the Chinese and as early as 1720 by MEISSEN. A brown is also employed, and in 1817 the MEISSEN factory invented a chrome-green which is found in the well known grape-pattern decorations. It is interesting to note that the limitations of underglaze colors make it necessary to decorate most porcelains on the glaze. The decorations are fused in or on the glaze during the second firing.

Vitreous Wares	A modern term applied to hard nonporous wares used in hotels and restaurants. It is composed of about 15 per cent feldspar, 38 per cent flint, 6 per cent ball clay, 40 per cent kaolin and 1 per cent whiting, and is fired at about 2300° F, making a "stony" type of vitrification rather than a "glassy" type.
Watteau Paintings	Paintings by the Frenchman Antoine Watteau (1684–1721) which were frequently copied in decorating porcelain during the middle of the 18th century. Watteau paintings are primarily of Regence style and are characterized by gentle and colorful figures and groups usually in landscape settings. Watteau was only one of several famous painters whose pictures suggested porcelain decorations.
Wedgwood Relief	A relief or projection of figures or ornaments where the raised parts and ground are of different colors — the relief usually being white and the ground blue. This combination was first made in the famous WEDGWOOD factory by Josiah Wedgwood (1730—95), the founder of the English ceramics industry. It has been employed subsequently by several other factories in Germany and elsewhere.
Zwiebelmuster	A German word meaning "onion pattern" and customarily referred to as such by English-speaking peoples. The underglaze blue decorations do not depict onion flowers as commonly believed. Instead, the leaves, blossoms and globular fruits of peonies and asters of *Indianische Blumen* are employed. The well-known *Meissener Zwiebelmuster* was introduced by Höroldt and has been a popular pattern in the MEISSEN and some other factories up to the present time. Sometimes the *Zwiebelmuster* is decorated with red and gold and perhaps other colors on the glaze.

INDEX

239

241